Contents

What you need to know about the National Tests

Preparing and practising for the Science Test

Instructions

Test A (Levels 3–5)	1
Test B (Levels 3–5)	20
Test C (Level 6)	37
Answers	49
Determining your child's level	65
Marking Grid	66

What you need to know about the National Tests

KEY STAGE 2 NATIONAL TESTS: HOW THEY WORK

Pupils between the ages of 7 and 11 (Years 3–6) cover Key Stage 2 of the National Curriculum. In May of their final year of Key Stage 2 (Year 6), all pupils take written National Tests (commonly known as SATs) in English, Mathematics and Science. The tests are carried out in school, under the supervision of teachers, but are marked by examiners outside the school.

The tests help to show what children have learned in these key subjects. They also help parents and teachers to know whether children are reaching the standards set out in the National Curriculum.

Each child will probably spend around five hours in total sitting the tests during one week in May. Most children will do two papers in Science and three papers in Mathematics and English.

The school sends the papers away to external examiners for marking. The school will then report the results of the tests to you by the end of July, along with the results of assessments made by teachers in the classroom, based on your child's work throughout Key Stage 2. You will also receive a summary of the results for all pupils at the school, and for pupils nationally. This will help you to compare the performance of your child with that of other children of the same age. The report from your child's school will explain to you what the results show about your child's progress, strengths, particular achievements and targets for development. It may also explain how to follow up the results with your child's teachers.

In addition, the publication of primary school performance (or 'league') tables will show how your child's school has performed in the teacher assessments and tests, compared to other schools locally and nationally.

UNDERSTANDING YOUR CHILD'S LEVEL OF ACHIEVEMENT

The National Curriculum divides standards for performance in each subject into a number of levels, from one to eight. On average, children are expected to advance one level for every two years they are at school. By Year 6 (the end of Key Stage 2), your child should be at Level 4. The table on page iii shows how your child is expected to progress through the levels at ages 7, 11 and 14 (the end of Key Stages 1, 2 and 3).

Most children will take the two papers for Levels 3–5 in Science. The two papers will contain the same number of marks. Each paper will be 35 minutes long. Extension papers with Level 6 questions are available for exceptionally able pupils. However, answering questions on the extension paper will require some knowledge of the content of Key Stage 3 Science.

What you need to know about the National Tests

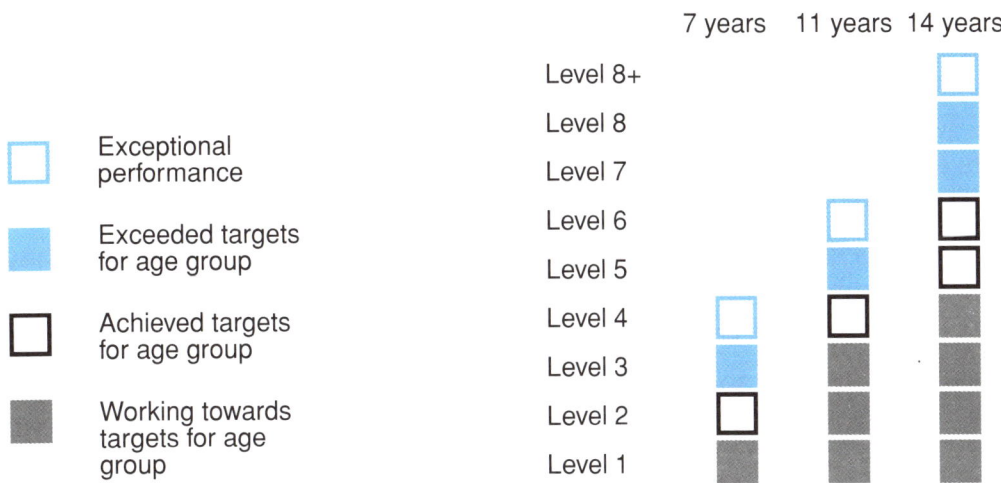

How your child should progress

This book concentrates on Levels 3–5, giving plenty of practice to help your child achieve the best level possible. There are also some Level 6 questions for very able pupils. Do not worry if your child cannot do these questions; remember that Level 4 is the target level for children at the end of Key Stage 2. The bar chart below shows you what percentage of pupils nationally reached each of the levels in the 1997 tests for Science.

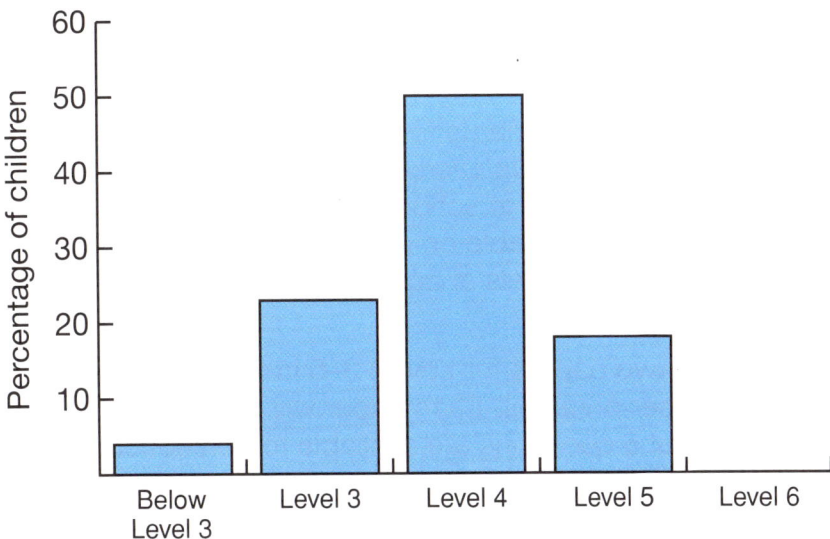

Levels achieved in Science, 1997

Preparing and practising for the Science Test

SCIENCE AT KEY STAGE 2

The questions in this book will test your child on the Key Stage 2 curriculum for Science. For assessment purposes, the National Curriculum divides Science into four sections, called Attainment Targets (ATs). The first AT, Scientific Investigation, is assessed only by the teacher in the classroom, not in the written tests. The other three ATs are:

AT2: Life Processes and Living Things (which is largely Biology)

AT3: Materials and their Properties (which is largely Chemistry)

AT4: Physical Processes (which is largely Physics)

The National Curriculum describes levels of performance for each of the four Science ATs. These AT levels are taken together to give an overall level for Science. The test papers have questions covering ATs 2–4. National Test questions are designed to assess your child's ability in four areas:

Knowledge and understanding

Handling information

Interpretation and evaluation

Problem solving

The questions in this book cover these skills.

USING THIS BOOK TO HELP YOUR CHILD PREPARE

This book contains four basic features:

Questions:	two test papers for Levels 3–5, and one extension paper for Level 6
Answers:	showing acceptable responses and marks
Notes to Parent:	giving advice on how to help your child avoid common mistakes and improve his or her score
Level Charts:	showing you how to interpret your child's marks to arrive at a level for each test, as well as an overall level

SETTING TESTS A AND B AT HOME

Try setting Test A first, mark it to see how your child has done, and work through the answers and advice together. Then set Test B on a different day. Let your child carry out the tests in a place where he or she is comfortable. Your child will need a pencil, a rubber and a ruler. In your own words, describe to your child how to work through the test. Make sure to work through the instructions on page vi together.

Note the starting time in the box at the top of each test. During the test, if your child cannot read a word you may read it out. If he or she does not understand a word, you can explain what the word means, providing it is not a scientific word.

Preparing and practising for the Science Test

For example, you can explain what is meant by the word 'label' but not 'force' or 'evaporate'.

After 45 minutes, ask your child to stop writing. If he or she has not finished, but wishes to continue working on the test, draw a line to show how much has been completed within the test time. Then let your child work to the end of the test.

SETTING TEST C

Test C is an extension paper, designed for exceptionally able children. Like the actual extension test, the questions on Test C are at Level 6 and require knowledge from both the Key Stage 2 and Key Stage 3 Programmes of Study. This means that most 11-year-olds will not yet have covered all the Science topics tested here. Your child should attempt Test C only if the results of Tests A and B suggest that he or she is working at Level 5 or higher. Test C should take 40 minutes. If your child is not ready to attempt this test, you may decide to make use of the material by working through some of the questions together.

MARKING THE QUESTIONS

When your child has completed a test, turn to the Answers section at the back of the book. Work through the answers with your child, using the Notes to Parent to help give advice, correct mistakes and explain problems. If your child required extra time to complete a test, go through all the questions with your child, but do not include the marks for the 'extra' questions in the total scores.

Using the recommended answers, award your child the appropriate mark or marks for each question. In the margin of each test page, there are small boxes divided in half. The marks available for each question are at the bottom; write your child's score in the top half of the box.

Enter the total number of marks for each question on the Marking Grid on page 66. Then add them up to find the total for the test. Look at the charts on page 65 to determine your child's level for each test, as well as an overall level.

FINALLY, AS THE TESTS DRAW NEAR

In the days before the tests, make sure your child is as relaxed and confident as possible. You can help by:

- ensuring your child knows what test papers he or she will be doing;
- working through practice questions, and discussing which answers are right and why.

Although the National Tests are important, your child's achievement throughout the school year is equally important. Encourage your child to do his or her best without putting him or her under too much pressure. Many children look forward to tests, but it is natural that some may be nervous. Look out for signs of anxiety, such as changes in eating or sleeping habits, and reassure your child if he or she is worried about these tests.

Instructions

Tests A and B should each take about 45 minutes.

Read all the words carefully. Look at any diagrams or pictures which should help you.

The questions for you to answer are in blue boxes.

For example:

> **Give the names of the parts of a flower shown in the picture.**

Look for the ▭▷ to show you where to write your answer.

Remember to explain your answers if you are asked to do so.

After finishing a page, turn over to a new page without waiting to be told.

If a question is too hard, you should move on to the next question.

GOOD LUCK!

Test A

Start ☐   **Finish** ☐

1 Ali went to visit a nearby pond in a farmer's field.

Ali, the birds and fish are all living things.

a One food chain shown in the picture is:

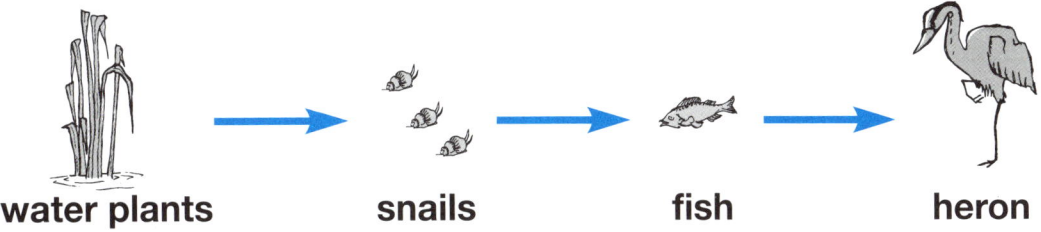

water plants   snails   fish   heron

Write down the name of the producer in this food chain.

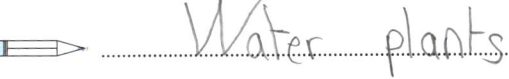
Water plants

b Pollution of the pond kills all of the fish.

What might happen to the heron?

It will not have any food. (Die out)

c Look back at the picture of the pond again.

Finish another food chain.

TEST A
LEVELS 3–5

MARKS

1
Q1a

1
Q1b

3
Q1c

TEST A
LEVELS 3–5

MARKS

Test A

d Tick **THREE** boxes to show **THREE** things Ali, the birds and fish must do to stay alive.

eat food ☐

lay eggs ☐

swim ☐

breathe ☐

fly ☐

lose waste materials ☐

3
Q1d

e Ali turned over a large stone. Underneath the stone he found a number of woodlice.

Write down THREE reasons why woodlice would prefer to live under the stone rather than on the surface of the earth.

1 ....

2 ....

3 ....

3
Q1e

2

Test A

2 The picture shows plants growing around an oak tree. Oak trees grow new leaves in spring and shed them in autumn.

a | **Why are there few plants growing in the shaded ground under the tree? Write down TWO reasons.**

1 ....

2 ....

b Bluebells are woodland plants that grow and flower in spring. They die down again in summer.

| **Write down ONE way in which the bluebell is suited to its environment.**

....

c The bird in the drawing is a woodpecker. Woodpeckers eat insects.

| **Write down ONE way in which the woodpecker is suited to its environment.**

....

d The leaf litter in the wood is home to many animals and micro-organisms.

| **What important job do the micro-organisms in the leaf litter do?**

....

TEST A
LEVELS 3–5

MARKS

2 Q2a

1 Q2b

1 Q2c

1 Q2d

TEST A
LEVELS 3–5

MARKS

3 The drawing shows some organs in the body.

The organs are:

brain   heart   kidney   lung   stomach

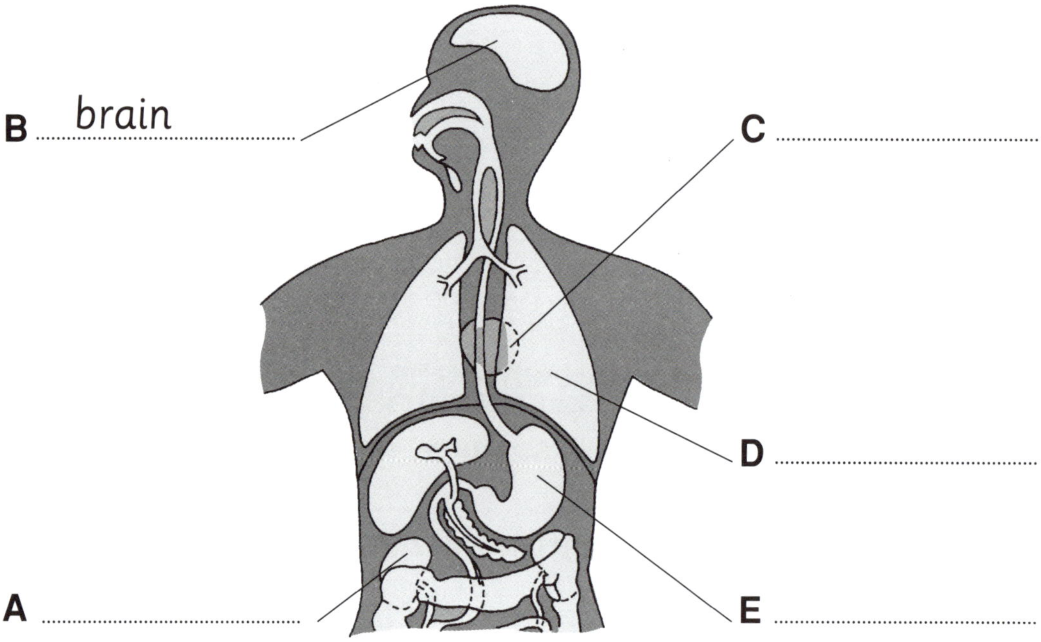

B ..... brain

A .....   C .....

D .....

E .....

4
Q3a

a Add labels to the organs labelled A, C, D and E on the diagram. One example, B, has been done for you.

b Each of the body organs has a job to do. Write the **LETTER** of the correct organ next to its job in the table below.

Job	Organ
pumps the blood round the body	
digests food	
filters the blood	
exchanges gases	
controls the body's actions	

5
Q3b

4

Test A

4 The graph shows how the height of a girl changes from the age of five to eighteen years old.

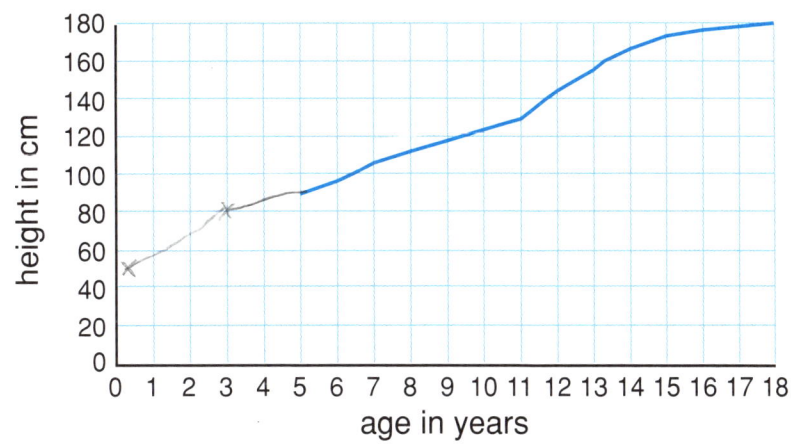

a How tall was the girl when she was nine years old?

b How much did she grow between her fifth and eleventh birthdays?

c How old was she when she started to grow faster?

d When she was born the girl was 50 cm tall. Put an X on the graph to show this.

e On her third birthday the girl was 80 cm tall. Put an X on the graph to show this.

f Draw a line through the crosses and join it to the line on the graph. Did she grow faster between birth and three years old or between three and five years old?

Test A

TEST A
LEVELS 3–5

MARKS

5 Sunil's mother tells him that she is pregnant, and he will be having a new brother or sister.

The words in the list describe the stages that the new baby will go through in its life.

adolescence   childhood   infancy   middle age
old age   young adulthood

a Arrange the list in the correct order, starting when the baby is born.

....
....

1
Q5a

b At which stage in the list is Sunil most likely to have a child of his own?

....

1
Q5b

c During which stages will Sunil's new brother or sister be growing taller?

....
....

1
Q5c

Test A

6a When water is left in an open dish, the water slowly disappears. Put a ring round the best word for the process taking place.

dissolving   distilling   drying   evaporating   melting

b Mel and Sue are comparing how long it takes for water to disappear from different-shaped containers.
The diagram shows the containers they use.

Choose words from this list to name the other containers in the diagram.

beaker   measuring cylinder   dish   test tube

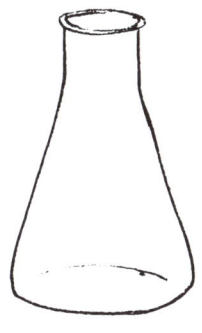

flask   ....

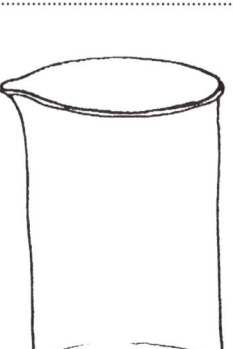

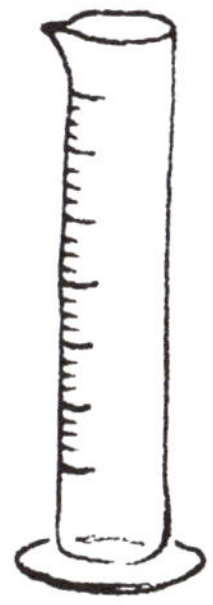

....

c Write down two things they should do to make a fair test.

1 ....

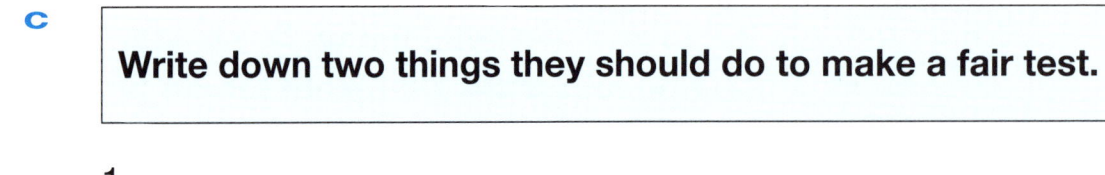

2 ....

d Why did they find that water disappeared faster from the dish than from the other three?

....

MARKS

7 Copper, paint, plastic, rubber and steel are used when cars are made.

Tick the box which shows why car makers use these materials.

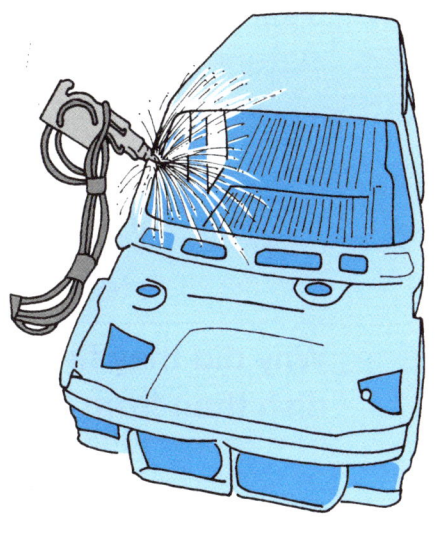

a Electric wiring in the car is made from **copper** because copper

- [ ] ... is shiny.
- [ ] ... is not magnetic.
- [ ] ... is a conductor of electricity.

1 Q7a

b Car tyres are made of **rubber** because rubber

- [ ] ... is black.
- [ ] ... is squashy.
- [ ] ... is made from the sap of the rubber tree.

1 Q7b

c Car steering wheels can be made of **plastic** because plastic

- [ ] ... is easily shaped.
- [ ] ... is heavy.
- [ ] ... does not conduct electricity.

1 Q7c

8 Here are some materials which may be used in making a car. Some of these materials are **natural** and some have been **made**.

Tick ONE box for each material to show if it is made or natural.

	Natural	Made
glass	☐	☐
steel	☐	☐
water	☐	☐
plastic	☐	☐
wood	☐	☐

9 The table shows some properties of solids, liquids and gases.

Property	Solid	Liquid	Gas
hard	yes	no	no
can flow easily	no	yes	yes
can be squashed easily	no	no	yes

Use the table to finish these sentences. One has been done for you.

The door handle of a car is made of a ___solid___

because _the handle is hard and cannot be squashed._

a The oil in the car engine is a _____

because _____

b The car tyre is filled with _____

because _____

10 The picture shows five liquids in their containers.

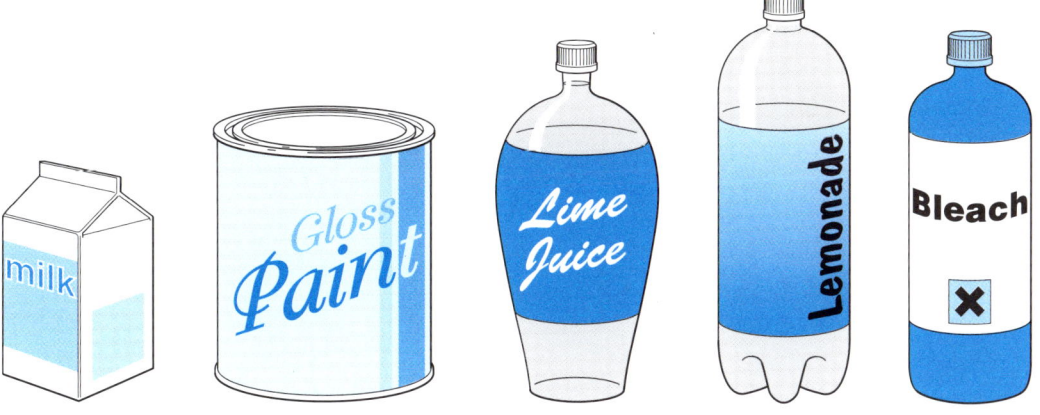

a

Write down THREE materials used to make these containers.

....

3
Q10a

b Some of the **liquids** are see-through and others are not see-through.

Finish the table. One has been done for you.

See-through	Not see-through
	bleach

2
Q10b

Letts

MARKS

Test A

11 A spoonful of blue crystals is added to cold water.

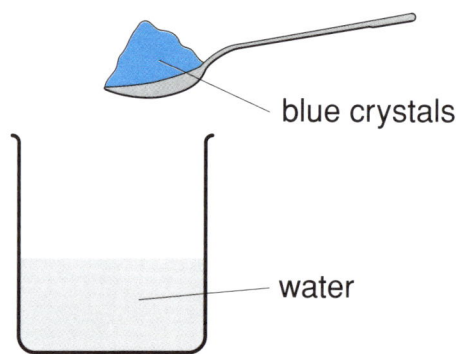

The crystals dissolve and form a solution. When no more crystals will dissolve, a <u>saturated</u> solution is left.

a **Write down <u>TWO</u> ways of dissolving the crystals more quickly.**

1 ....

2 ....

2 Q11a

b **How does this solution look different from water?**

....

1 Q11b

A hot saturated solution is allowed to cool.

c **What will be formed?**

....

1 Q11c

d **How will the result be different if the solution is cooled quickly?**

....

1 Q11d

Letts

e   Diagram 1 shows the hot saturated solution being cooled quickly.
Diagram 2 shows another way of cooling the solution.

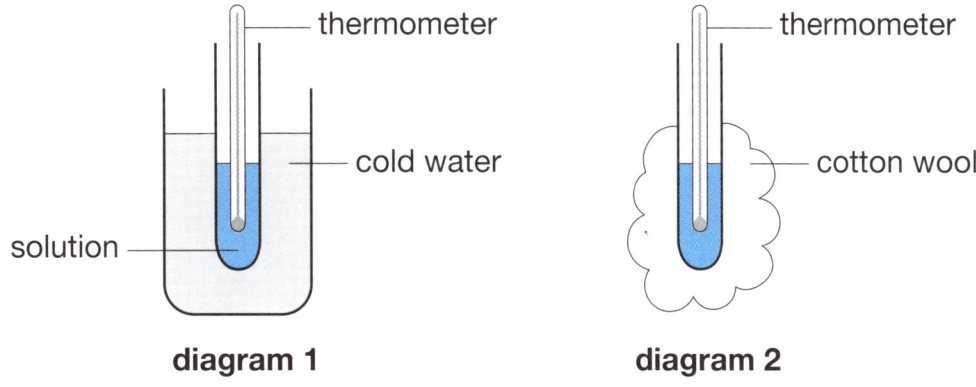

The solution in diagram 1 was left to cool for 10 minutes.

The graph shows changes to the temperature of the solution.

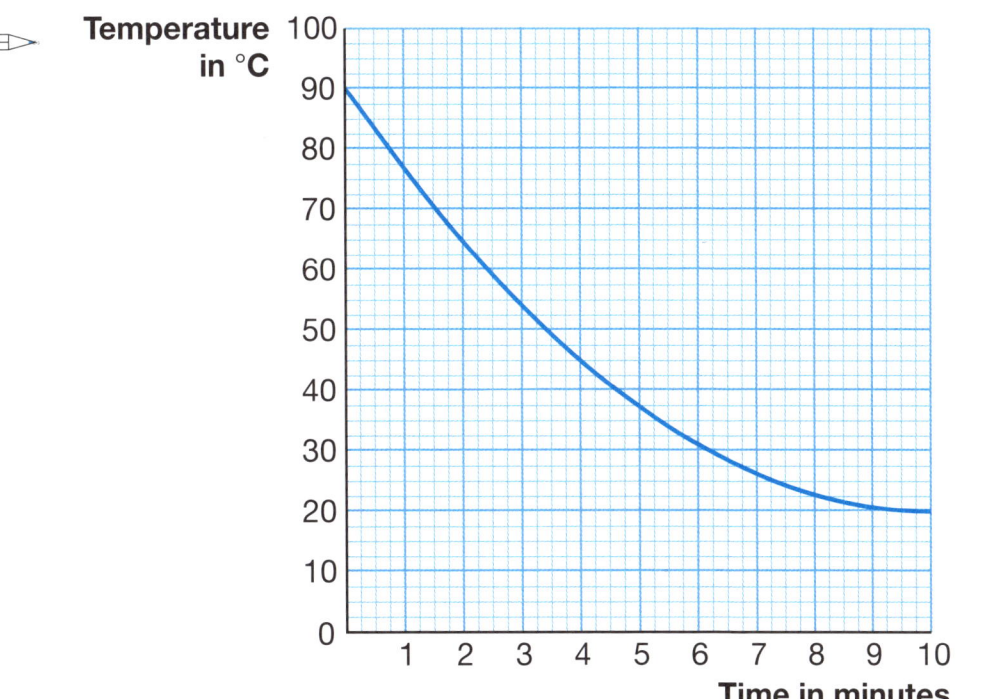

The solution in diagram 2 was left to cool for 10 minutes.

Draw a different line on the graph to show the changes to the temperature of the solution in diagram 2.

12 Some children record the position of the Sun from their classroom window.

The drawing shows the position of the Sun in the morning and afternoon of a day in winter.

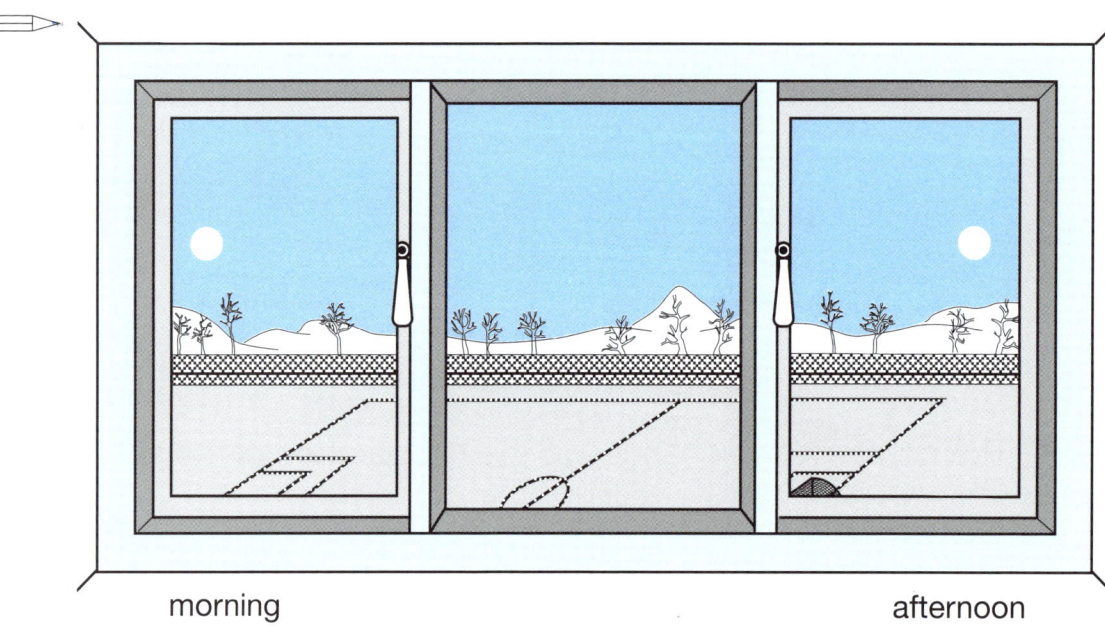

morning   afternoon

a **Draw a circle to show where they would see the Sun at midday.**

b The children track the Sun by marking the shadow of a pole in the playground. The drawing shows the shadow in the morning.

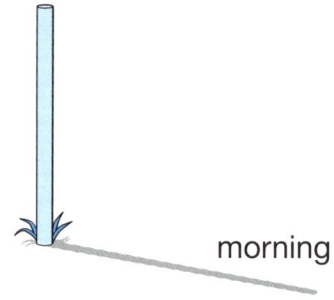

morning

Draw and label the shadows they would see at midday and in the afternoon.

13 The drawing shows the Earth, the Sun and the Moon.

Not to scale

a **Shade in the part of the Earth where it is night.**

b During the next twenty-four hours the night changes to day and back to night.

Explain what causes this.

....

....

14 Sandy is making a model to show how the Sun, Earth and Moon are arranged.

Choose the objects she should use by placing a tick next to the best choice in each column in the table.

Sun	Earth	Moon
cushion	tennis ball	apple
cardboard box	bag of sugar	sugar cube
football	sugar cube	football
apple	grape	table-tennis ball

MARKS

Test A

15 There was a full Moon on 25 May.

Underline the possible date of the next full Moon after this.

1 June **9 June** **16 June** **23 June**

1
Q15

16 In autumn, leaves fall from the trees.

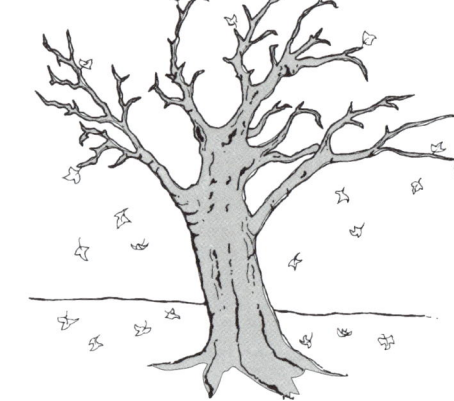

a **Write the name of the force that pulls the leaves down.**

....

1
Q16a

b As the leaves fall another force pushes up on them.

What force pushes up on the leaves?

....

1
Q16b

17 A small girl sits on a swing.

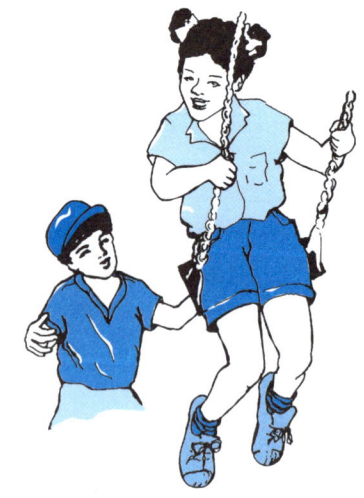

Write down <u>TWO</u> ways in which her brother can make the swing move.

1 ....

2 ....

2
Q17

18 Claire throws her ball straight up into the air.

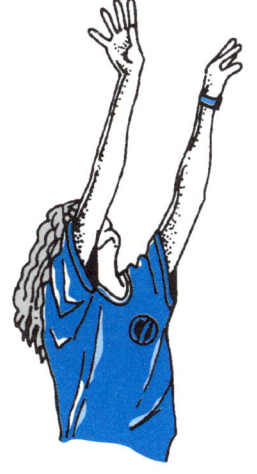

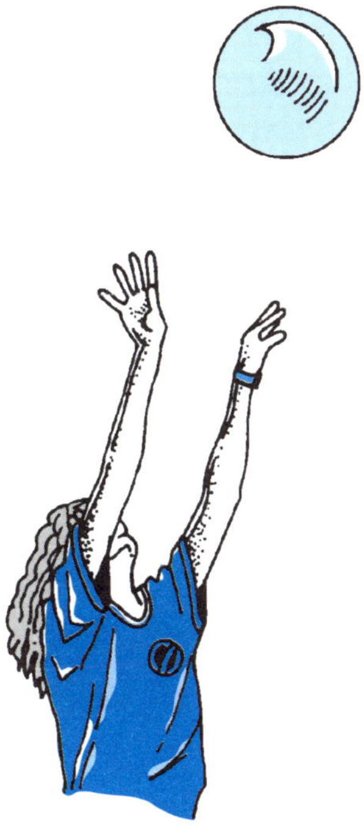

a **What happens to the speed of the ball as it goes up?**

....

1 Q18a

b **Why does the ball fall down again?**

....

....

1 Q18b

c The **Earth's pull** and **air resistance** act on the ball as it falls down.

Mark these forces on the drawing of the ball falling down. Use an arrow labelled E for the Earth's pull and an arrow labelled A for air resistance.

2 Q18c

d **Which force is bigger, the Earth's pull or air resistance?**

....

1 Q18d

e **How could you tell that this force is bigger?**

....

1 Q18e

TEST A
LEVELS 3–5

MARKS

1 Q19a

3 Q19b

1 Q20a

1 Q20b

Test A

19 Robert is walking in the park holding a balloon. The balloon is filled with helium.

Helium is a gas which is lighter than air.

One force on the balloon has been marked on the drawing.

a **What will happen to the balloon if Robert lets go of it?**

b **Explain why this will happen.**

20 A child is playing on a bouncy toy in the park.

a **What happens to the spring when the child sits on it?**

b **Why does this happen?**

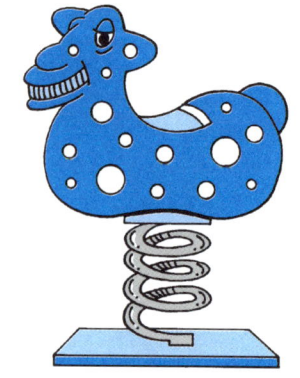

18

MARKS

21 Sam builds a toy car and puts a magnet on it.

He finds that he can **push** the car along by holding another magnet near to it.

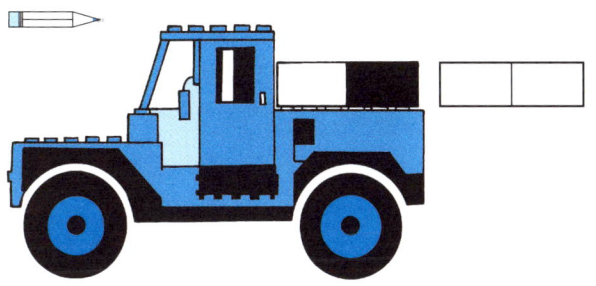

a **Draw an arrow on the car to show which way it moves when it is pushed by the magnet.**

1 Q21a

b **Shade the right-hand magnet to show how Sam must hold it so that it pushes the car.**

1 Q21b

c Sam uses a magnet to pick up a paper clip. The arrow on the drawing shows the force that is pulling the paper clip down.

Draw an arrow to show the other force on the paper clip.

1 Q21c

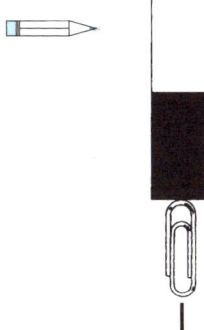

Sam places two magnets on a table with a paper clip between them.

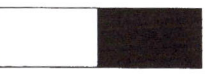

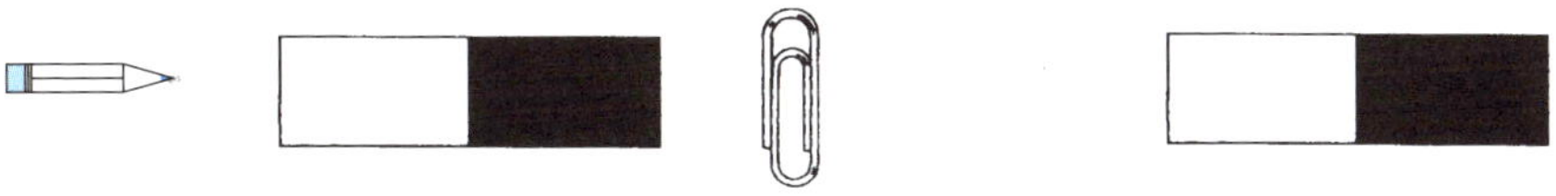

d **Draw arrows on the paper clip to show the pulls from the magnets.**

2 Q21d

e **Which way does the paper clip move?**

....

1 Q21e

f **Where should Sam put the paper clip so that it does not move? Draw it on the picture above.**

1 Q21f

TEST B
LEVELS 3–5

MARKS

Test B

| Start | | Finish | |

1 Ian found three small animals and used a key to find out what they were.

Here is the key.

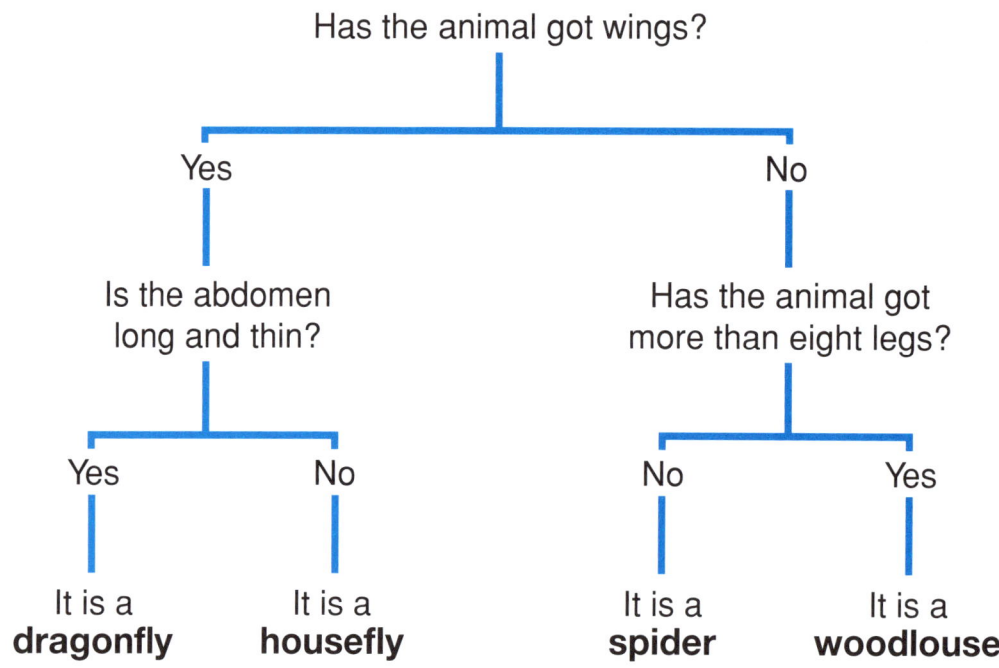

Write the names of the three small animals Ian found underneath the pictures.

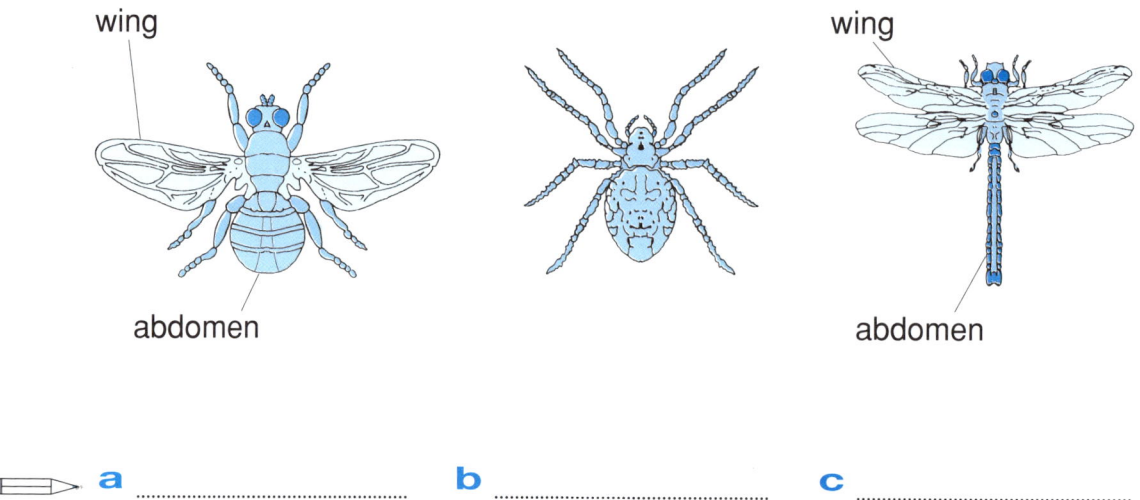

3
Q1

a .... b .... c ....

Test B

2 The diagram shows a bean plant.

a Add labels to the diagram above, using words from the list below.

flower   fruit   leaf   roots   seed   stem

b Write down the letter A, B, C or D which gives the part of the plant which has seeds inside.

....

c Write down the letter A, B, C or D which shows the part of the plant which takes in water.

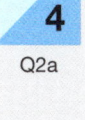

....

Test B

3 The diagram shows some of the parts of a flower.

a **Fill in the box with the name of the part of the flower.**

....

1
Q3a

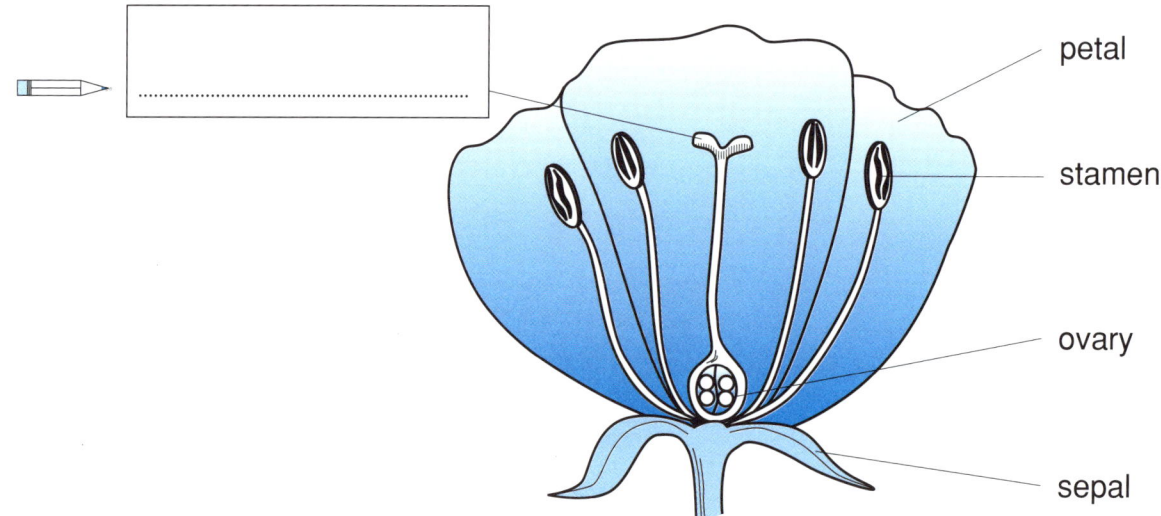

b Here are two lists. The first is a list of parts of a flower. The second is a list of jobs that different parts of a flower do.

Part of flower	**Job**
petal	protect the bud
ovary	attract insects for pollination
stamen	produce egg cells
sepal	produce pollen

Draw a line to join each part of a flower to its job. One has been done for you.

3
Q3b

Test B

TEST B
LEVELS 3–5

MARKS

4   The drawing shows some of the teeth in your mouth.

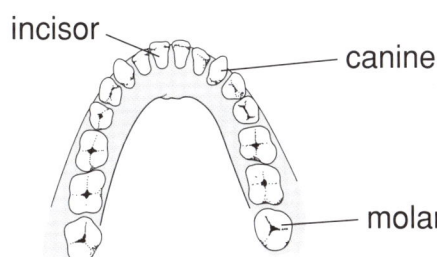

a   **Write down the job of each type of tooth.**

➡ incisor ....

➡ canine ....

➡ molar ....

3
Q4a

b   **Which type of tooth has sharp edges?**

➡ ....

1
Q4b

c   The picture shows a mouth.

Plaque on teeth is a mixture of food, microbes and acids.

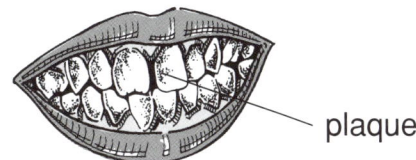

Why is it important to remove plaque from teeth?

➡ ....

1
Q4c

d   **How can plaque be removed from teeth and gums?**

➡ ....

1
Q4d

e   **When are the best times of day to remove plaque from teeth?**

➡ ....

1
Q4e

23

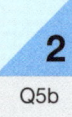

5 The drawing shows an organ system.

a **Which organ system is shown in the drawing?**

....

b **Explain why it is important to pump blood around the body.**

....

....

c Blood travels to the leg muscles in an **artery** and returns to the heart in a **vein**.

Describe TWO differences between the blood in the artery and the blood in the vein.

....

....

6 As part of a science experiment, Jemma is fitted with a device that measures her pulse rate throughout the day.

The chart shows Jemma's pulse rate at playtime.

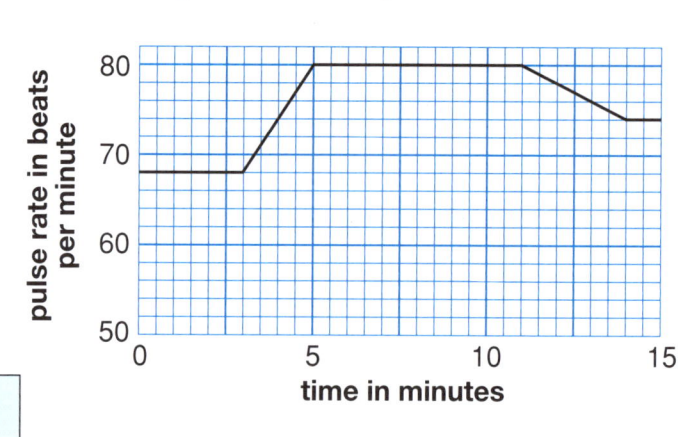

a **What is a pulse rate?**

....

Test B

b At the beginning of playtime, Jemma sat down to have a drink and an apple.

> How long did Jemma spend sitting down?

....

c After having her drink, Jemma played football with her friends.

> How can you tell when Jemma started to play football?

....

d Eleven minutes into playtime, Jemma's pulse rate started to go down.

> Suggest why this happened.

....

e > What was Jemma's pulse rate at the end of playtime?

....

7a > Finish the sentences by filling in words from the following list.

    burns   combustion   energy   evaporation
        melts   oxygen   waste gases

A fuel is a material which .... to release

.... and produce ....

When a fuel burns it uses up ....

from the air.

Another word for burning is ....

TEST B
LEVELS 3–5

MARKS

The service station sells different fuels.

b | **Write down the name of a solid fuel, a liquid fuel and a gas fuel sold at the service station.**

Solid fuel .... Liquid fuel ....

Gas fuel ....

2
Q7b

c Here are two lists. The first is a list of raw materials and the second is a list of products made from them. All of the products are seen in the service station.

| **Draw a line to join each of the materials to the product made from it. One has been done for you.** |

Raw material	Product
iron ore	glass
clay	petrol
sand	charcoal
wood	bricks
crude oil	steel girders

4
Q7c

d | **Why is a ban on smoking important in a service station?**

....

1
Q7d

e When petrol is spilled it smells strongly and soon disappears.

| **An oil spill does not smell and does not disappear. Explain these differences.** |

....
....

2
Q7e

26

MARKS

8 The diagram shows some ice cubes in a fizzy drink in a glass.

a **What happens to the ice cubes in a fizzy drink over a long period of time?**

....

....

1 Q8a

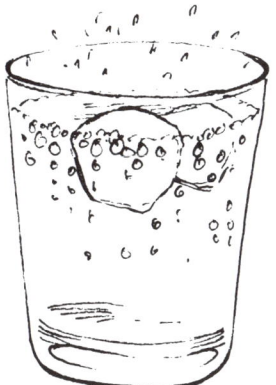

b **Explain why water droplets form on the outside of the glass.**

....

....

2 Q8b

9 The diagram shows part of the water cycle.

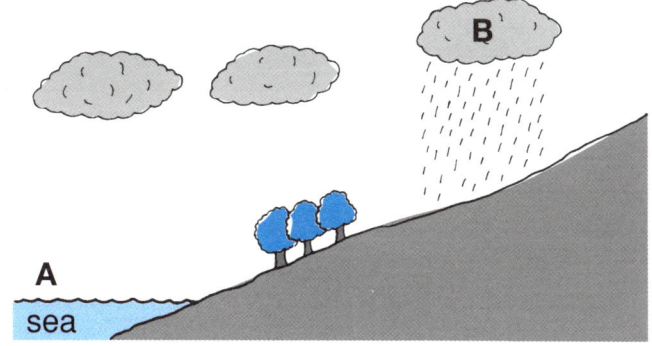

a **What is happening at points A and B on the diagram?**

A ....

B ....

2 Q9a

b **Draw an arrow on the diagram to show one other way that water leaves the Earth and forms clouds.**

1 Q9b

MARKS

Test B

10 A test was carried out to compare three duvets, **A**, **B**, and **C**, to find out which one would keep in the heat best.

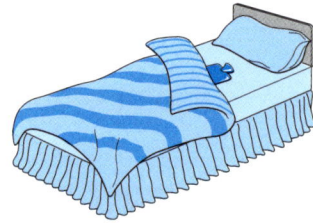

A hot-water bottle was filled with boiling water and placed on a bed under one of the duvets. After four hours, the bottle was removed and the temperature of the water measured. This was repeated with the other duvets. The results were:

Duvet	Temperature after four hours
A	55°C
B	58°C
C	65°C

a **What would you use to measure the temperature of the water after four hours?**

....

1 Q10a

b **Why does the temperature of the water in the bottle drop?**

....

1 Q10b

c **Which duvet is the best? Explain your answer.**

Duvet ....

....

2 Q10c

d **Suggest THREE things which should be done to make sure it is a fair test.**

1 ....

2 ....

3 ....

3 Q10d

Letts

MARKS

11 Here are some materials we use.

paper

wood

iron

polythene film

limestone rock

aluminium foil

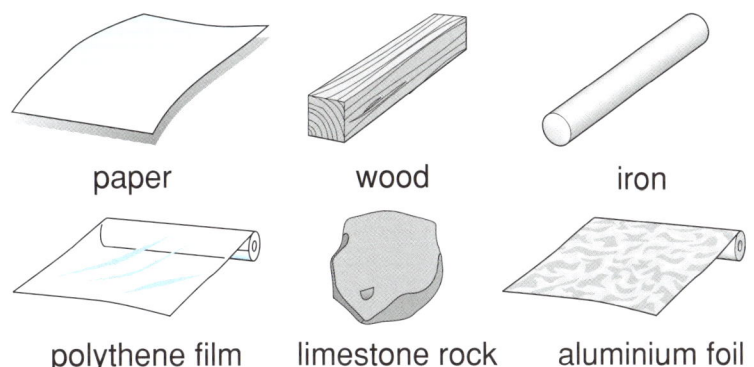

a **Finish the table showing some of the properties of these materials.**

Material	Easy to bend	Attracted to a magnet	Hard	See-through
wood	✗	✗	✗	✗
paper	✓	✗	✗	✗
iron				
polythene				
limestone				
aluminium foil				

4 Q11a

b **Write down THREE of these materials which burn when heated in a flame.**

1 ....

2 ....

3 ....

3 Q11b

c **Write down ONE material which melts when heated in a flame.**

....

1 Q11c

12 Here are three circuits which each have two bulbs and two switches.

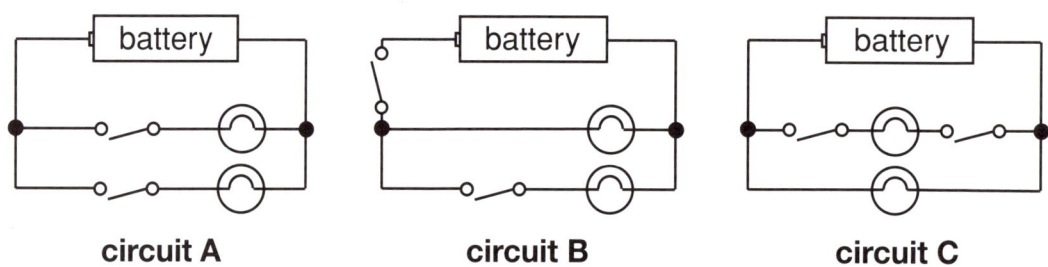

circuit A circuit B circuit C

a In which circuit does each bulb have its own switch?

....

b Which has a bulb that is *on* when both switches are *off*?

....

c Which **TWO** circuits have a bulb that only lights up when *both* switches are *on*?

....
....

13 Here is a circuit with two batteries and a bulb.

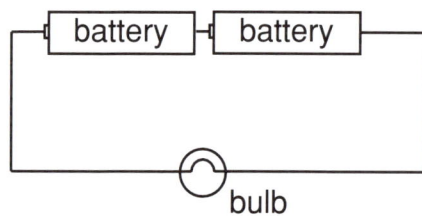

a Write down one way of making the bulb brighter.

....

Test B

b What must happen to the current to make the bulb brighter?

....

c Write down one way of making the bulb dimmer, apart from removing a battery.

....

14 The diagrams each show a bulb, a battery and two switches.

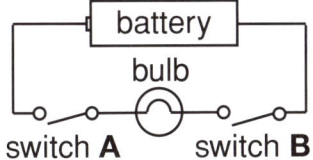

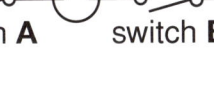

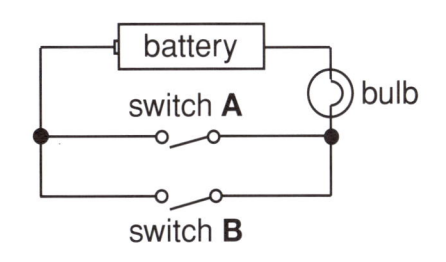

circuit 1   circuit 2

a Finish the tables to show when each bulb is *on* or *off*.

Circuit 1			Circuit 2		
Switch A	Switch B	Bulb on or off	Switch A	Switch B	Bulb on or off
off	off		off	off	
on	off		on	off	
off	on		off	on	
on	on		on	on	

b Finish the sentences by filling in the missing words.

To light the bulb in circuit 1, switch A .... switch B need to be pressed.

To light the bulb in circuit 2, switch A .... switch B needs to be pressed.

31

15 The diagram shows a battery and a bulb.

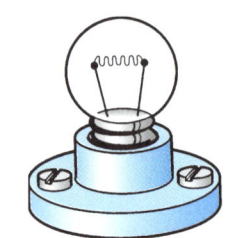

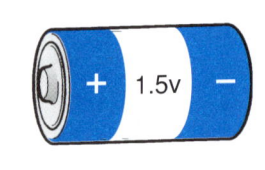

a Draw **TWO** wires on the diagram to show how you could make the bulb light up.

b This diagram shows a bulb and a motor.
The bulb is not alight.

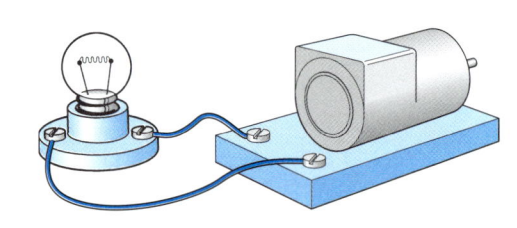

What else is needed to make the bulb light up?

....

c Draw a diagram of a circuit which could be used to make the bulb light up. You must use the circuit symbols from the table below.

Electrical item	Circuit symbol
bulb	—⊗—
battery	—∣⊢—
motor	—Ⓜ—

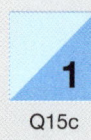

Test B

16 Sarah shines a torch at a mirror.

a **What happens to the light when it hits the mirror? Underline the best word.**

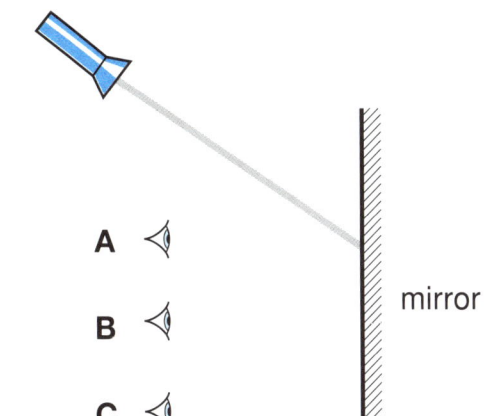

affected	deflected	reflected	tilted

b **Which eye in the drawing is in the best place to see the light after it hits the mirror?**

....

17 **Underline the things in the list that *give out* light.**

book	candle	mirror	radio	Sun	television

18 Ravi uses a torch and some cardboard shapes to make shadow pictures on a wall.

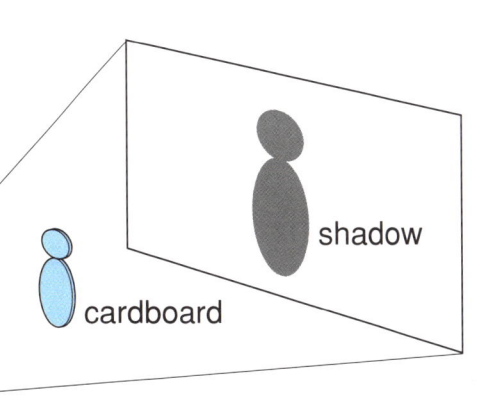

How does the size of the shadow change when the cardboard is moved?

....

....

TEST B
LEVELS 3–5

MARKS

Test B

19 After dark, Paula sits in her bedroom reading her book.

Explain how Paula sees her book.

....

....

....

....

3
Q19

20 Petra looks at a burning candle.

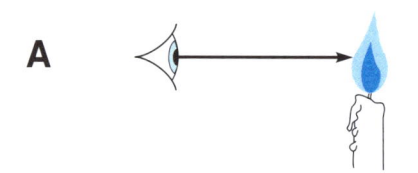

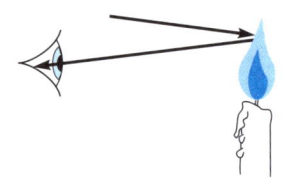

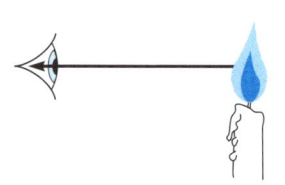

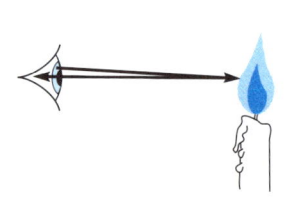

A
B
C
D

Which diagram shows how she sees the candle?

....

1
Q20

21 The Moon does not give out light.

Explain how, on a clear night, you can see the Moon.

....

....

2
Q21

34

22 When a note is played on a piano a hammer hits a string. This makes the string move.

The pictures show the movement of the string. The arrows show which way the string is moving.

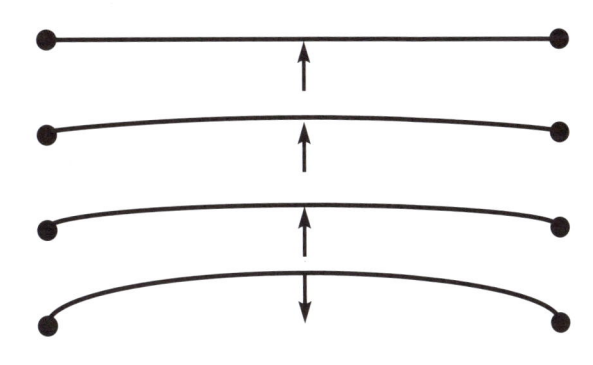

a Underline the word that *best* describes the movement of the string.

acceleration   rotation   vibration

b The strings on a piano each play a different note.

Write down **TWO** ways in which piano strings can be different from each other.

1 ....

2 ....

TEST B
LEVELS 3–5

MARKS

23 Tony makes a musical sound by blowing through a drinking straw.

a | How does the sound change when he cuts the end off the straw to make it shorter?

....

....

2
Q23a

b | What should Tony do to make the sound louder?

....

....

1
Q23b

c Tony's mother is in the same room as Tony, listening to him playing his toy.

| How does the sound travel from the straw to her ears?

....

....

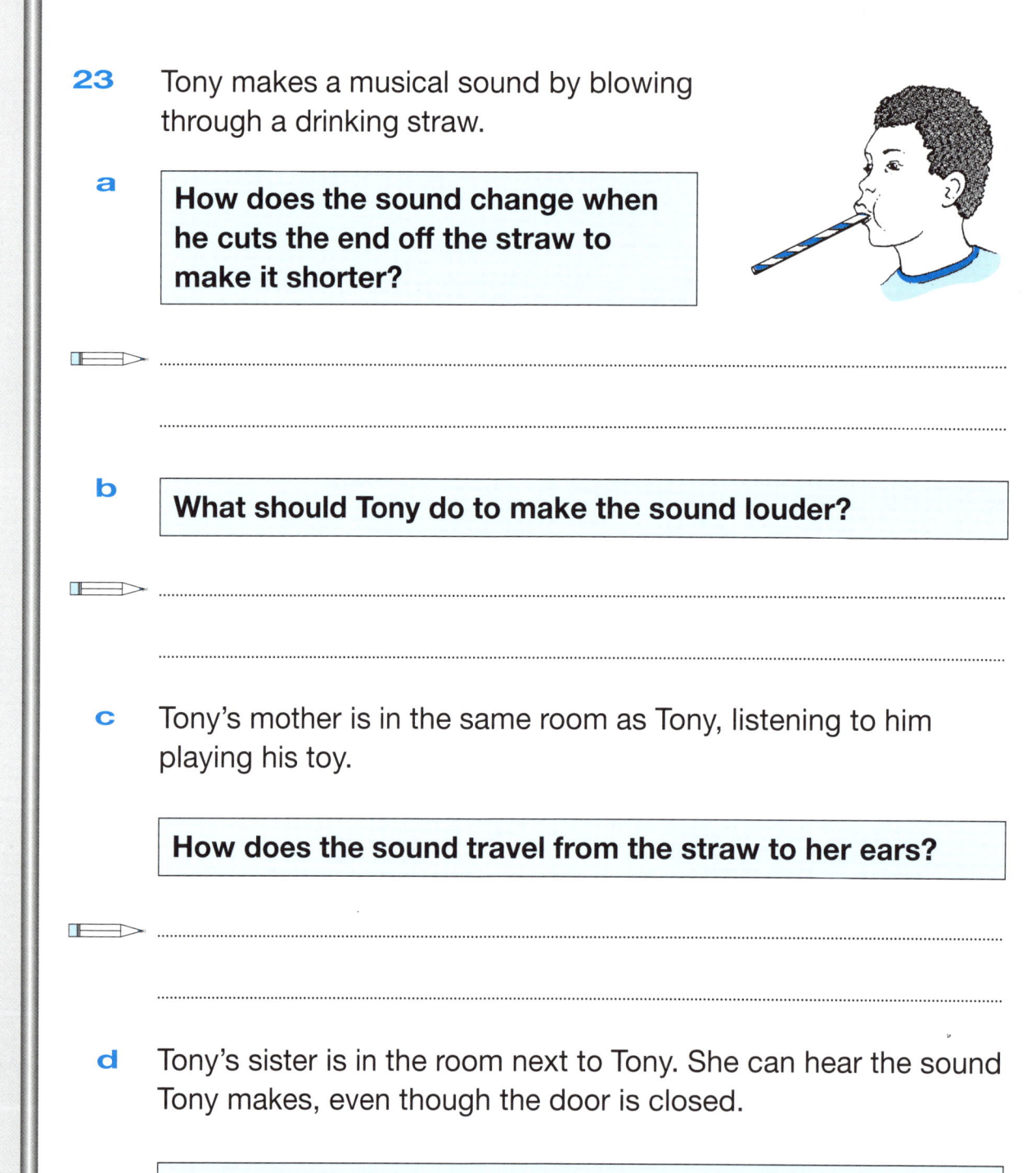

1
Q23c

d Tony's sister is in the room next to Tony. She can hear the sound Tony makes, even though the door is closed.

| Explain how Tony's sister can hear the sound.

....

....

1
Q23d

36

Test C
Level 6

> Test C is very challenging. Before you continue, make sure your parent has read the notes on page v about this test.

Start ☐   Finish ☐

1 Plants make their own food in a process called **photosynthesis**. The diagram illustrates photosynthesis.

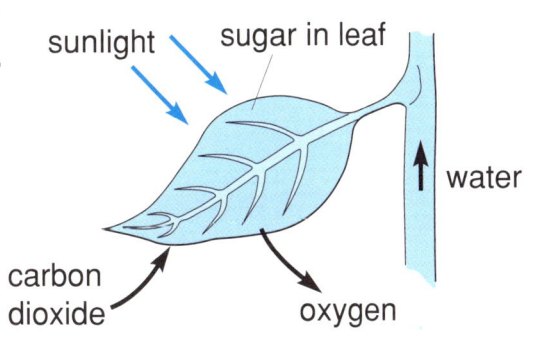

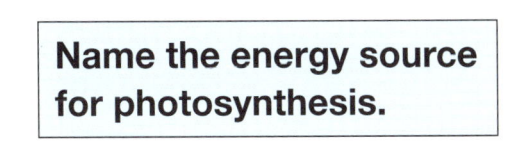

a Name the energy source for photosynthesis.

....

b Name the **TWO** substances that a plant uses to make food.

....

....

c Write down the name of the food that the plant makes.

....

d Write down **TWO** reasons why photosynthesis is important for all living things.

1 ....

2 ....

2 The diagram shows a plant cell.

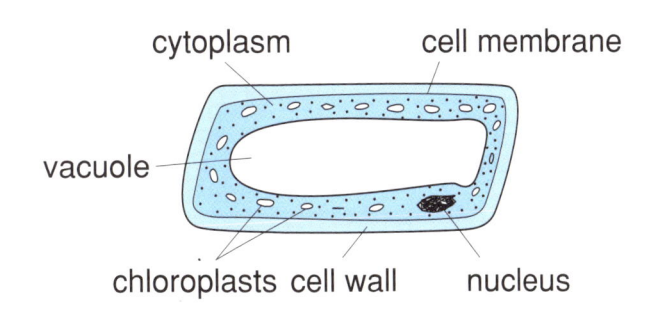

a Explain why a plant cell has a cell wall.

....

Test C
Level 6

b What important process takes place in the chloroplasts?

✎ ....

c What is the job of the nucleus?

✎ ....

d Draw and label a diagram of an animal cell.

✎

3 a Choose words to finish the sentence about breathing.

air   carbon dioxide   nitrogen   oxygen

✎ When we breathe in, ...

is taken into the lungs. The lungs

absorb .... and give

out waste ....

b Write down **TWO** changes that happen to blood as it passes through the lungs.

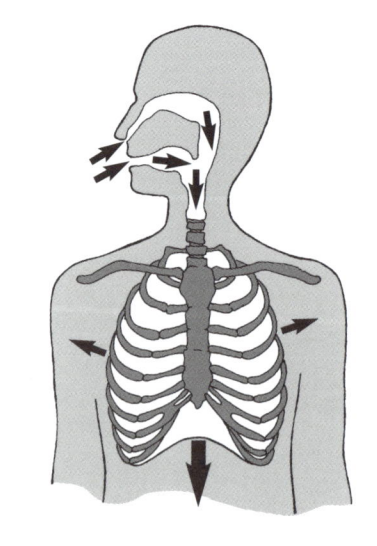

✎ 1 ....

✎ 2 ....

38

Test C
Level 6

4 A rusting experiment was carried out with three test tubes. Each test tube contained a steel nail.

The tubes were left for a week. The test tubes are shown in the diagram below.

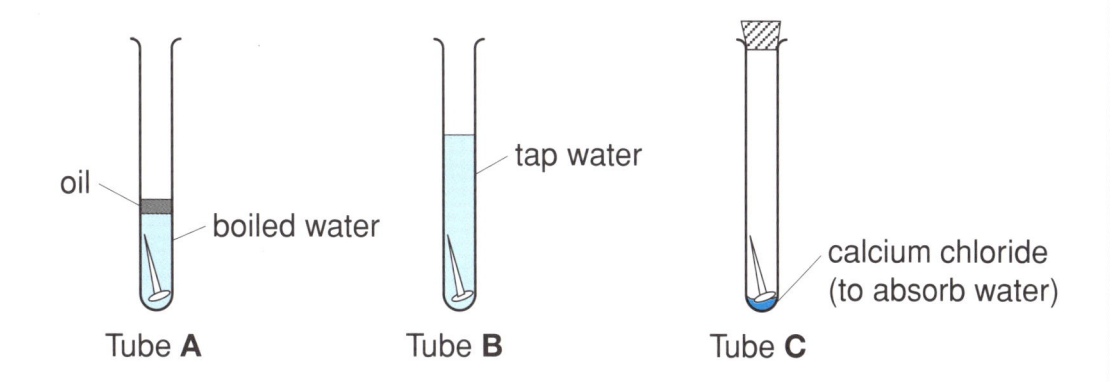

Tube **A**: oil, boiled water
Tube **B**: tap water
Tube **C**: calcium chloride (to absorb water)

After a week, only the nail in tube **B** had rusted.

a **Explain why rusting did not take place in tube A.**

....

....

b **Explain why rusting did not take place in tube C.**

....

....

Iron and steel can be painted to prevent rusting.

c **Apart from painting, write down TWO ways of preventing iron and steel from rusting.**

1 ....

2 ....

5 Write down **TWO** things needed for iron or steel to rust.

1 ....

2 ....

6 Rock salt is put onto the roads during the winter to melt ice and snow.

What problem does this cause for car owners?

....

....

....

7 Animals and plants both **respire**. Energy for movement comes from respiration in the muscles.

Choose words from the list to answer **a** and **b**.

    carbon dioxide   chlorophyll   glucose   nitrogen
    oxygen   starch   water

a Name the **TWO** substances that muscles use when they respire.

1 ....

2 ....

b Name the TWO waste products of respiration.

1 ....

2 ....

c Describe how each of the waste products is removed from the body.

....

....

8 Copper oxide is formed when copper carbonate is split up by heating. Carbon dioxide is also produced.

a Underline the type of reaction taking place when copper carbonate is heated.

combustion   oxidation

reduction   thermal decomposition

b Write a word equation for the reaction taking place.

| .... | → | .... | + | .... |

c When hydrogen is passed over heated black copper oxide, a reaction takes place. The word equation for the reaction is:

copper oxide + hydrogen → copper + hydrogen oxide

Some copper oxide weighing 4 g is turned into copper.
The mass of the copper is

| exactly 4 g | more than 4 g | less than 4 g |

Put a ring around the best answer.

d Some magnesium ribbon is burned in a dish.

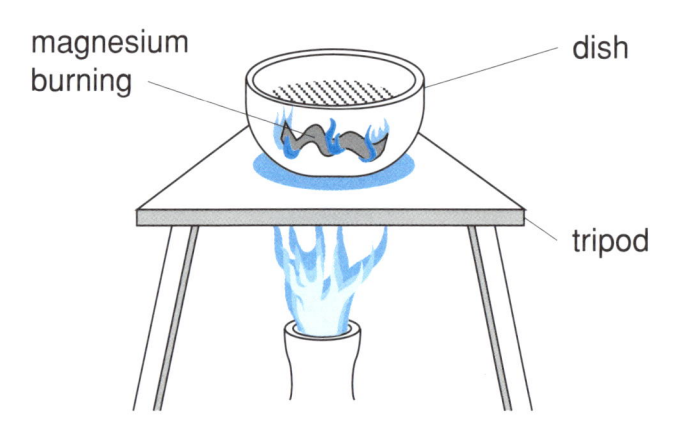

At the end, the ash remaining weighs *more* than the magnesium ribbon weighed at the start.

Why does the ash weigh more than the magnesium?

....

9 Iron and sulphur are **elements**.

When iron is burned in oxygen, iron oxide is formed.
Iron oxide has a pH value of 7.

When sulphur is burned in oxygen, sulphur oxide is formed.
Sulphur oxide has a pH value of 4.

Test C
Level 6

a **What does this information tell you about iron and sulphur?**

✎ iron ....

✎ sulphur ....

b Iron and sulphur powders can be mixed together to give a **mixture** of iron and sulphur.

How could iron be separated from this mixture?

✎ ....
....

c When a mixture of iron and sulphur is heated a chemical reaction takes place.

Give the name of the compound formed.

✎ ....

d In the diagram below:

- ● stands for an iron atom;   ● stands for a sulphur atom.

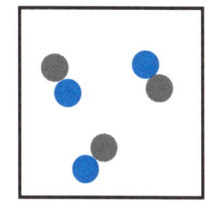

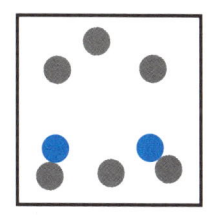

A   B   C

Choose which letter, A, B or C, represents the following.

✎ A mixture of iron and sulphur ....

✎ A compound of iron and sulphur ....

10 Children in the same class at school can be very different in height, as the drawing shows.

Write down TWO reasons which could explain why Darren is taller than Paul.

1 ....

2 ....

11 Three rocks in the Earth are shown in the list.

granite   limestone   marble

a **Which one of these rocks is formed when liquid rock in the Earth crystallises?**

....

b **Which one of these rocks is formed by the action of high pressures and high temperatures on existing rocks?**

....

Test C
Level 6

12 The diagram shows two carbon rods connected to a battery. The carbon rods are in blue copper sulphate solution. The solution contains both positively and negatively charged particles.

a What would you see happening at the negative electrode during the experiment?

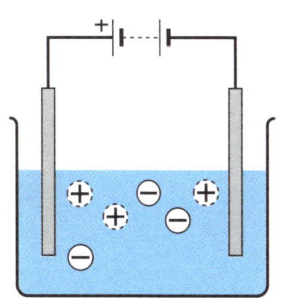

....

b What would you see happening to the solution during the experiment?

....

13 The diagram shows a circuit with a bulb and a motor.

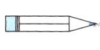

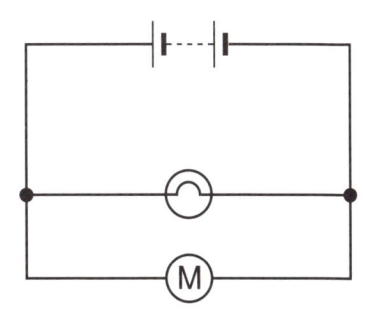

a Mark an A in a position where you would place an ammeter to measure the current in the bulb only.

b Mark a B in a position where you would place an ammeter to measure the total current in the motor and the bulb.

14 The arrows show the horizontal forces on a car travelling forwards on a level road.

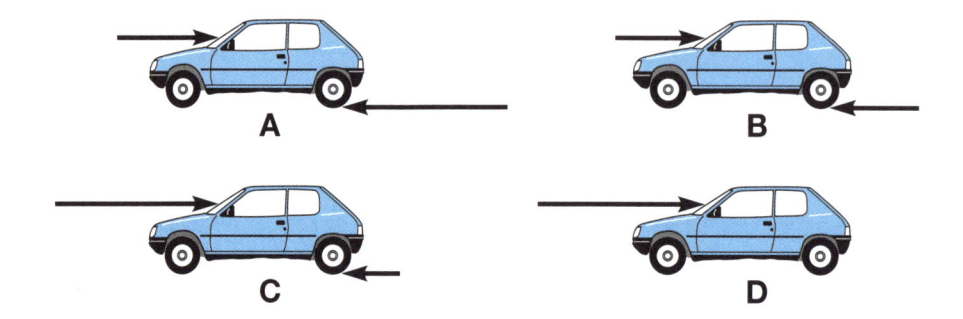

A   B

C   D

a **Which diagram or diagrams show a car that is:**

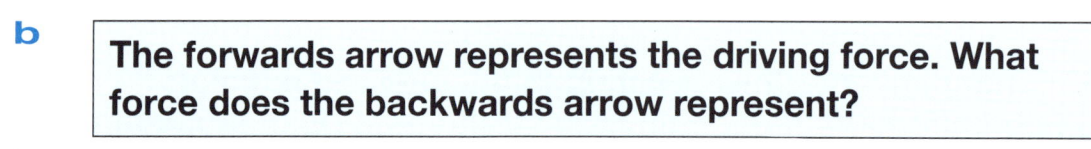

✏ speeding up? ....

✏ slowing down? ....

✏ travelling at a steady speed? ....

b **The forwards arrow represents the driving force. What force does the backwards arrow represent?**

✏ ....

c When the car travels onto a patch of mud, the wheels spin round but the car does not move forwards.

Explain why the car does not move forwards.

✏ ....

15 The drawing shows the positions of the three planets that are closest to the Sun.

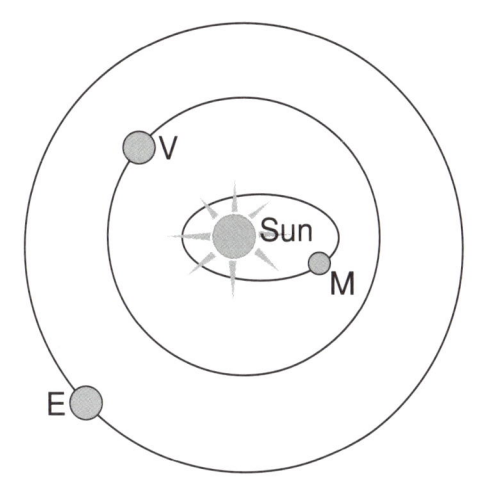

a Write down **TWO** differences between the orbit of planet M and the orbit of planet V.

1 ....

2 ....

b The times taken by the planets to orbit the Sun are shown in the table.

Orbit time	Planet
88 Earth days	
365 Earth days	
225 Earth days	

Write the letter of the correct planet next to its orbit time.

16 When light passes through glass it is **refracted**.

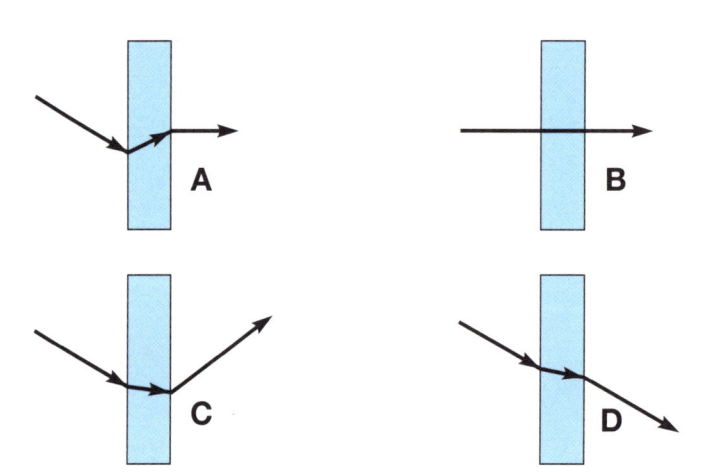

Which diagrams show how light travels through a window?

....

17 Rainbows are sometimes seen when light passes through drops of water.

Tick the statement which explains how rainbows are formed.

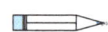

A The water drops add different colours to the light. ☐

B Light looks different colours when it is wet. ☐

C The water drops split the white light into different colours. ☐

D The water drops take colours out of the light. ☐

Answers

HOW TO MARK THE QUESTIONS

When marking your child's test remember that the answers given are sample answers. You must look at your child's answers and judge whether they deserve credit. Award the mark if the answer deserves credit.

You should pay special attention to spelling. Look at any misspelt word as written and read it aloud. If it sounds correct and has the correct number of syllables, the mark can be awarded. For example, 'desolv' and 'wait' are acceptable as alternatives to dissolve and weight. However, 'photosis' is not correct as an alternative to photosynthesis.

Encourage the correct spelling of scientific words. Look through this book and make a list of scientific words correctly spelt. Reviewing this list in the days before the tests is good preparation for your child.

It is sometimes difficult to know what children mean by their answers. Often, a vague use of the word 'it' can cause confusion. For example, if asked to explain how the experiment showed that Duvet C was warmest, a child may write 'it did not get very cold'. This answer does not make clear whether 'it' refers to Duvet C or the hot-water bottle which retained its heat longest when kept under Duvet C. An ambiguous answer must be marked wrong. When discussing these answers, encourage your child to be very clear about what he or she means, and to replace the word 'it' with the subject in full.

Above all, as you go through the test with your child, try to be positive. Look for good things that have been done in addition to resolving errors.

Enter your child's marks for each test on the Marking Grid on page 66, and then work out your child's level of achievement on these tests on page 65.

Test A — Pages 1–19

1 a Water plants — *1 mark*
  b The heron could die but it is more likely that the heron would move elsewhere to find food. — *Either answer: 1 mark*
  c Grass → rabbit → stoat *or* man — *3 marks*
  d Eat food
     Breathe
     Lose waste materials
     Award three marks if all correct and none incorrect.
     Award two marks if two correct and one wrong.
     Award one mark if one correct and two wrong. — *3 marks*
  e Cool
     Damp
     Safe from predators
     Supply of food
     Dark *or* not in direct light
     Any three: one mark each — *3 marks*

Total 11 marks

> **Note to parent**
>
> There may be other answers to **e**. You need to look at the answer and award marks if it seems reasonable.

Test A Answers

2	**a**	There is not much light.		*1 mark*
		There is not much water.		*1 mark*
	b	They grow and flower in spring, when there is the most light under the trees.		*1 mark*
	c	Its long, pointed beak enables it to eat insects hidden in holes in the bark.		*1 mark*
	d	They rot the leaves or cause them to decay.		*1 mark*

Total 5 marks

Note to parent

In part **a**, accept 'lack of nutrients' as one alternative answer, but not 'lack of food'.

3 a A kidney — *1 mark*
    C heart — *1 mark*
    D lung — *1 mark*
    E stomach — *1 mark*
  b C — *1 mark*
    E — *1 mark*
    A — *1 mark*
    D — *1 mark*
    B — *1 mark*

Total 9 marks

4 a 119 cm – Allow answer between 118 cm and 120 cm. — *1 mark*
  b 40 cm – Allow answer between 38 cm and 42 cm. — *1 mark*
  c 11 — *1 mark*
  d x at 0 years and 50 cm — *1 mark*
  e x at 3 years and 80 cm — *1 mark*
  f A line drawn over the whole time from birth to five years. — *1 mark*
    Between birth and three years. — *1 mark*

Total 7 marks

Note to parent

The steeper line between birth and three years shows that the girl was growing faster. This question tests your child's skill in handling data. This is an important scientific skill that is tested in KS2 tests.

5 a Infancy, childhood, adolescence, young adulthood, middle age, old age — *1 mark*
  b Young adulthood — *1 mark*
  c Infancy, childhood and adolescence — *1 mark*

Total 3 marks

6 a Evaporating — *1 mark*
  b Measuring cylinder, beaker, dish — *3 marks*
  c Equal volumes (masses) of water, same length of time, same temperature. (*Any 2*) — *2 marks*

Note to parent

Other answers include 'same humidity', 'same draught'. Try to avoid the ambiguous word 'amount'.

  d The water has a larger surface in contact with the air (for evaporation to take place). — *1 mark*

Note to parent

This important idea explains why large, shallow puddles evaporate faster than small deep ones.

Total 7 marks

Test A Answers

> **Note to parent**
>
> This question is testing your child's understanding of the processes of filtration and distillation but in a slightly different context. Distillation involves two processes – boiling followed by condensation.

7 **a** is a conductor of electricity. *1 mark*
    b is squashy. *1 mark*
    c is easily shaped. *1 mark*
Total 3 marks

> **Note to parent**
>
> These questions are designed to get your child to pick a reason why certain materials are used for certain jobs. You will notice in **a**, for example, that all three possible answers are correct descriptions of copper, but it is important to pick the reason which fits. With electric wiring, obviously electrical conductivity is essential.

8 'Made' boxes should be ticked for glass, steel, plastic.
'Natural' boxes should be ticked for water and wood.
Award one mark for each correct answer. Do not award a mark for answers where both 'Made' and 'Natural' boxes are ticked for one material. *5 marks*
Total 5 marks

> **Note to parent**
>
> If your child has made the common mistake of ticking both boxes for one material, remind him or her of the importance of following the instructions then checking.

9 **a** liquid *1 mark*
       because it can flow easily *1 mark*
    b gas *1 mark*
       because it can be squashed easily *1 mark*
Total 4 marks

> **Note to parent**
>
> This question requires your child to use information in the table and not just to recall the properties of solids, liquids and gases. With **a** there is no problem as only one property is suitable but in **b** a correct choice has to be made.

10 **a** Glass, plastic (or the name of a plastic, e.g. polythene), metal (or the name of a metal, e.g. steel), cardboard (or waxed paper)
Award one mark for each correct answer up to a maximum of three. *3 marks*

Test A Answers

b

See-through	Not see-through
lemonade	*bleach*
lime juice	milk
	gloss paint

2 marks
Total 5 marks

Note to parent

There are four answers here. Award half a mark for each correct answer and round up the nearest whole number. For example, three correct = one and a half marks but round up to two.

Note carefully here that the question is about whether the liquids and not the containers are see-through. The word transparent has not been used but it is a useful word for your child to know.

11 a Any two of the following:
    Heat the water.
    Stir the mixture.
    Grind up the crystals into a fine powder.
    Use a larger volume of water. *2 marks*
b The solution is blue in colour. *1 mark*
c Crystals (accept solid). *1 mark*

Note to parent

The idea that 100g of a solvent can only dissolve a certain mass of solute *at a particular temperature* is important and frequently misunderstood. It is called a *saturated* solution.

d The crystals will be smaller in size. *1 mark*
e The diagram shows a suitable response.
In marking you should look for three things.
The line drawn must start at the same point as the original line, i.e. 90°C.
The line must be less steep than the original line and must never cross the original line or go up or level off.
The line should stop at exactly 10 minutes.
You should award 1 mark for each of the above points to a maximum of 3.

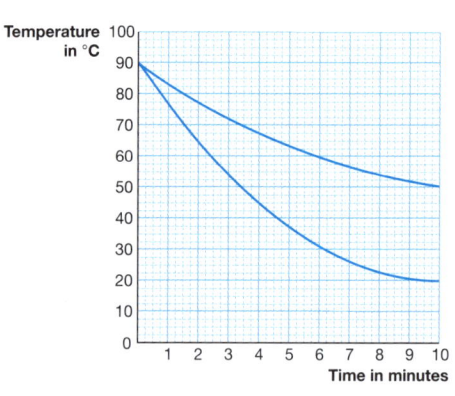

3 marks
Total 8 marks

Note to parent

The marking of this kind of sketch graph is very tight. A sharp pencil is needed and some practice to try and draw a steady line does help. In this question your child is expected to realise that the solution in diagram 2 will cool more slowly than the solution in diagram 1. The temperature must never go up. Stopping the line exactly at 10 minutes shows your child has followed the instructions exactly.

Test A Answers

12 a The circle should be between the two in the drawing, and higher up. *1 mark*
b

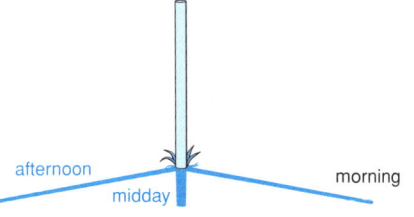

afternoon — midday — morning

Award one mark for each shadow drawn correctly. *2 marks*
Total 3 marks

> **Note to parent**
>
> This question is testing whether your child knows that when the Sun is low in the sky the shadows are long and they become shorter as the Sun gets higher.

13 a The right-hand part of the Earth should be shaded. *1 mark*
b The Earth turns round *or* spins *or* rotates *1 mark*
on its own axis. *1 mark*
Total 3 marks

14 Sun: a football *1 mark*
Earth: a tennis ball *1 mark*
Moon: a table-tennis ball *1 mark*
Total 3 marks

> **Note to parent**
>
> This question is testing whether your child is aware of the relative sizes of the bodies, as well as the spherical shape.

15 23 June *1 mark*
Total 1 mark

16 a The Earth's pull *or* gravity *or* the weight of the leaves *1 mark*

> **Note to parent**
>
> Children often talk about gravity as if it were an object. To avoid confusion, they should be encouraged to use the phrase 'the Earth's pull'.

b Air resistance *1 mark*
Total 2 marks

17 Push it *1 mark*
Pull it *1 mark*
Total 2 marks

18 a It gets less *or* it slows down. *1 mark*
b The Earth (*or* gravity) pulls it. *1 mark*
c E pointing downwards *1 mark*
A pointing upwards *1 mark*
d The Earth's pull *1 mark*

Test A Answers

e	The ball speeds up as it falls.	1 mark
		Total 6 marks

Note to parent

Do not give a mark for 'because it is falling down'. The direction of travel does not give any information about the relative sizes of the forces.

19	a	It will go up.	1 mark
	b	Awareness that there is an upward force.	1 mark
		Awareness that there is a downward force.	1 mark
		The upward force is bigger.	1 mark
			Total 4 marks

Note to parent

Your child could answer this question at one of three levels. A simple answer such as 'because there is a force pushing it up' would gain one mark, whereas a fully correct answer 'the upward force is bigger than the downward force' gains three marks.

20	a	It becomes small *or* it is squashed.	1 mark

Note to parent

The question is testing whether the child knows that the shape of the spring changes, so do not give the mark for 'it moves down'.

	b	Because of the force pushing it down *or* the weight of the child.	1 mark
			Total 2 marks

21	a	The arrow should point from right to left.	1 mark
	b	The left-hand side of the magnet should be shaded.	1 mark
	c	An arrow pointing up	1 mark
		This arrow represents the upward pull of the magnet.	
	d	One arrow to the left ←	1 mark
		One arrow to the right →	1 mark

Note to parent

This question is testing the direction of the forces; the relative size of the arrows does not matter here.

	e	To the left	1 mark
	f	Paper clip drawn in the centre of the gap between the magnets.	1 mark
			Total 7 marks

TOTAL FOR TEST A 100 marks

Test B Answers

| Test B | Pages 20–36 |

1 **a** Housefly — *1 mark*
    b Spider — *1 mark*
    c Dragonfly — *1 mark*

Total 3 marks

Note to parent

Being able to use keys is an important scientific skill at this level. Your child will not be expected to construct a key in a KS2 test but will be expected to use one as we have done in this question. It is worthwhile spending some time drawing up a simple key with your child so that he or she understands the principles.

Take four ordinary household objects, e.g. a cup, saucer, drinking glass and plastic measuring jug. Look at the similarities and differences, e.g. material used to make them, use, whether or not they have a handle, whether they can be used to measure, etc. Then draw up a key and check that the key enables you to identify each object individually. To understand the principles you do not have to use complicated objects. Then get your child to make up one alone. Check it at the end.

2 **a** **A** – Roots **B** – Stem **C** – Fruit **D** – Leaf — *4 marks*

Note to parent

At first sight you might think it strange to call the bean a fruit. Biologists have a slightly different use of the word 'fruit' from the general public. The biological definition of a fruit is a fertilised ovary. It may not be edible. In the case of the bean the fertilised ovary becomes fleshy and can be eaten. In biological terms tomatoes and cucumbers are fruits. Fruits contain seeds.

    b **C** – The fruit — *1 mark*
    c **A** – The roots — *1 mark*

Total 6 marks

3 **a** Stigma — *1 mark*

Note to parent

Children frequently write 'sigma' for this. It is an unacceptable answer.

    b Ovary – produce egg cells — *1 mark*
        Stamen – produce pollen — *1 mark*
        Sepal – protect the bud — *1 mark*

Total 4 marks

4 **a** Incisor: cuts food — *1 mark*
       Canine: rips or tears food — *1 mark*
       Molar: grinds food into small pieces — *1 mark*
    b Incisor — *1 mark*

Note to parent

Canine teeth are also sharp but they have points rather than edges.

Test B Answers

    c To prevent gum disease (Accept 'to prevent tooth decay')   *1 mark*
    d By brushing with toothpaste   *1 mark*
    e Before breakfast and before bedtime   *1 mark*
    Total 7 marks

5 a The circulatory system   *1 mark*

> **Note to parent**
>
> Only give your child the mark if he or she has written 'circulatory' or 'circulation', but do not penalise spelling. Pupils working at Level 4 are expected to use scientific terms for major body organs.

    b It takes oxygen and food to different parts of the body.   *1 mark*
        It removes waste products from body organs.   *1 mark*
    c The blood in the artery:
           has more oxygen
           has more food
           has less carbon dioxide or other waste materials
           is at a higher pressure
        Any two   *2 marks*
    Total 5 marks

> **Note to parent**
>
> These differences apply to most, but not all, arteries and veins.

6 a The number of heartbeats in a certain time. For example, 70 beats per minute   *1 mark*

> **Note to parent**
>
> The idea of rate is an important one in Science. Here is a good way to introduce it. It is important to stress it is the number of heartbeats in a unit of time. You could show your child how to find his or her own pulse in the wrist or neck, measure pulse rate and do some simple experiments.

    b 3 minutes   *1 mark*
    c Her pulse rate starts to go up.   *1 mark*
    d She stopped playing football or started to rest.   *1 mark*
    e 74 beats per minute.   *1 mark*
    Total 5 marks

> **Note to parent**
>
> As well as testing whether your child understands how pulse rate is linked to rest and exercise, this question tests his or her skills in reading data from a graph.

7 a burns; energy; waste gases; oxygen; combustion   *One mark for each answer: 5 marks*
    b Solid fuel – charcoal *or* coal
        Liquid fuel – petrol diesel *or* paraffin
        Gas fuel – camping gas
        All three correct: 2 marks; two correct: 1 mark   *2 marks*
    c Lines from clay to bricks, sand to glass, wood to charcoal, crude oil to petrol
        One mark for each answer: 4 marks
    d Petrol is very flammable or catches fire easily.   *1 mark*

Test B Answers

	e	Petrol evaporates much faster than oil.	*1 mark*
		The vapour causes the smell.	*1 mark*
			Total 14 marks

Note to parent

This question is testing whether your child knows that the 'disappearance' of the liquid is due to evaporation and that liquids with strong smells evaporate readily.

8 a The ice cubes melt. — *1 mark*
  b Water vapour in the air comes into contact with the cold surface, — *1 mark*
     water vapour condenses into water droplets on the outside of the glass. — *1 mark*
     Total 3 marks

Note to parent

The correct use of scientific words is important at Key Stage 2. Your child must use the words 'melt' and 'condense' in his or her answer.

9 a A – evaporation — *1 mark*
     B – precipitation (*or* raining *or* snowing) — *1 mark*
  b Arrow from trees *or* ground to clouds — *1 mark*
     Total 3 marks

10 a Thermometer — *1 mark*
   b Energy is lost as heat through the duvet (and through the bed) — *1 mark*
   c Duvet C — *1 mark*
      The temperature fell less with C than with A or B — *1 mark*

Note to parent

This question requires your child to use the results in the table. It does not require any knowledge. He or she should be looking for the one which loses the least amount of heat, shown by the smallest drop in temperature.

  d *Any three of the following:*
      Use the same volume (or mass) of boiling water.
      Use the same hot-water bottle.
      Use the same bed.
      Make sure the room temperature is the same each time. — *3 marks*
      Total 7 marks

Note to parent

Your child should be familiar with the idea of fair testing when doing practical investigations. This involves keeping all of the factors the same, except one which is varied. In this case everything should be the same except for the duvet. However, the question states that boiling water is used each time and so keeping the temperature of the water constant is not an acceptable answer.

Test B Answers

11 a

Material	Easy to bend	Attracted to a magnet	Hard	See-through
wood	✗	✗	✗	✗
paper	✓	✗	✗	✗
iron	✗	✓	✓	✗
polythene	✓	✗	✗	✓
limestone	✗	✗	✓	✗
aluminium foil	✓	✗	✗	✗

There are sixteen answers. Award:
4 marks if 13–16 are correct
3 marks if 10–12 are correct
2 marks if 7–9 are correct
1 mark if 4–6 are correct — *4 marks*

b Polythene, paper and wood — *1 mark each in any order: 3 marks*
c Polythene — *1 mark*
Total 8 marks

12 a A — *1 mark*
b C — *1 mark*
c B and C — *One mark each: 2 marks*
Total 4 marks

13 a Add another battery to the circuit. — *1 mark*
b It increases. — *1 mark*
c Either add another bulb or a variable resistor in series. — *1 mark*
Total 3 marks

14 a Circuit 1: off, off, off, on — *2 marks*
Circuit 2: off, on, on, on — *2 marks*
b and — *1 mark*
or — *1 mark*
Total 6 marks

15 a One wire should be drawn from the + side of the battery to one side of the bulb. A second wire should lead from the – side of the battery to the other side of the bulb. — *1 mark*
b A battery — *1 mark*
c The correct symbols should be drawn in series or parallel, e.g.:

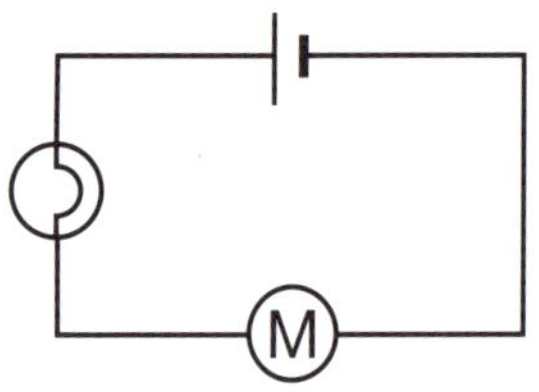

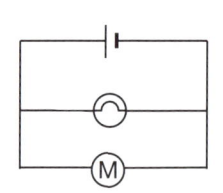

— *1 mark*
Total 3 marks

Note to parent
The answer is wrong if the symbols are incorrect, e.g.  or if there are gaps in the circuit, e.g.

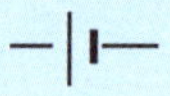

Test B Answers

16 a Reflected — *1 mark*
  b C — *1 mark*
  Total 2 marks

> **Note to parent**
>
> To get the correct answer in **b**, your child needs to recognise that the light is reflected at the same angle when it hits the mirror.

17 Candle, Sun and television — *1 mark*
  Total 1 mark

> **Note to parent**
>
> If your child answered 'mirror' this shows confusion between things that reflect light and sources of light.

18 As the cardboard moves closer to the screen — *1 mark*
  the shadow gets smaller. — *1 mark*
  Total 2 marks

> **Note to parent**
>
> Also accept 'As the cardboard moves closer to the torch, the shadow gets bigger'. There are two variables involved here: the distance from the cardboard to the screen (or torch) and the size of the shadow. The size of the shadow is a *dependent* variable. It depends upon the distance, which is the *independent* variable.

19 Light from the lamp reaches the book. — *1 mark*
  The book reflects light. — *1 mark*
  Light from the book enters the eye. — *1 mark*
  Total 3 marks

> **Note to parent**
>
> There are three important points to emphasise here: light travels out from a light source; surfaces reflect light; we see things when light from them enters our eyes.

20 C — *1 mark*
  Total 1 mark

> **Note to parent**
>
> This question is testing the first and last points emphasised in the note after Question 19.

21 Light comes from the Sun. — *1 mark*
  It is reflected by the Moon. — *1 mark*
  Total 2 marks

> **Note to parent**
>
> Your child may not appreciate that light comes from the Sun even at night. A model using a table lamp, a football and a tennis ball could help to explain this.

Test B Answers

22 a Vibration — *1 mark*
b *Two from:* longer/shorter; heavier/lighter; tighter/slacker — *One mark each: 2 marks*
Total 3 marks

> **Note to parent**
>
> Only award a mark for *one* of the answers from each pair given, e.g. do not award a mark for 'longer' and a mark for 'shorter'.

23 a The pitch changes. — *1 mark*
It becomes higher. — *1 mark*

> **Note to parent**
>
> Award your child the first mark for recognising that there is a change in pitch, even if he or she gives the wrong change; therefore 'it gets lower' is awarded one mark and 'it gets higher' is awarded two marks.

b Blow harder. — *1 mark*
c The sound travels through the air. — *1 mark*
d The sound travels through the walls or door. — *1 mark*
Total 5 marks

TOTAL FOR TEST B 100 marks

Test C Answers

Test C — **Pages 37–48**

1 a The Sun — *1 mark*
  b Carbon dioxide and water — *One mark each: 2 marks*
  c Sugar or glucose — *1 mark*
  d Any two of the following:
   It provides food for plants.
   Plants provide food for animals.
   It removes carbon dioxide from the atmosphere.
   It supplies oxygen to the atmosphere. — *One mark each: 2 marks*
   Total 6 marks

Note to parent
Children working at Level 6 should realise that photosynthesis is important in maintaining the balance of gases in the atmosphere and in providing the food source for all living things.

2 a The cell wall keeps the cell in shape or makes it strong. — *1 mark*

Note to parent
Children working at Level 6 should appreciate that plants depend on cell walls for their rigidity.

  b Photosynthesis — *1 mark*
  c The nucleus controls the cell. — *1 mark*
  d The important parts are: the cell membrane, the cytoplasm and the nucleus.

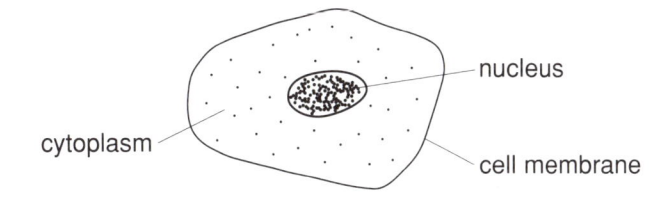

[Diagram of a cell with labels: nucleus, cytoplasm, cell membrane]

One mark for each correctly drawn and labelled: 3 marks
Total 6 marks

3 a Air
   Oxygen
   Carbon dioxide — *3 marks*
  b It loses carbon dioxide. — *1 mark*
   It gains oxygen. — *1 mark*
   Total 5 marks

Note to parent
Do not give a mark for 'it gains air', but do give a mark for 'it loses water' if your child gives this answer instead of one of those given.

Test C Answers

4 a Air (*or* oxygen) was removed from the water on boiling. — *1 mark*
Air (*or* oxygen) cannot get in through the oil. — *1 mark*
b Calcium chloride (or drying agent) removes water. — *1 mark*
Rusting does not take place in the absence of water. — *1 mark*
c Oiling, greasing, galvanizing (i.e. coating the steel with zinc), coating with plastic (e.g. washing-up racks), using a reactive metal such as magnesium in contact with the steel. (This is called sacrificial protecting as the magnesium corrodes in preference to the steel and is used to stop the legs of piers corroding.)
Any two answers: 2 marks
Total 6 marks

5 Oxygen *or* air — *1 mark*
Water *or* moisture — *1 mark*
Total 2 marks

6 Salt speeds up rusting and so can cause cars to rust faster. — *1 mark*
Total 1 mark

7 a Glucose and oxygen — *1 mark each: 2 marks*
b Water and carbon dioxide — *1 mark each: 2 marks*
c Carbon dioxide is removed by breathing. — *1 mark*
Water is removed in urine or by breathing or sweating. — *1 mark*
Total 6 marks

8 a Thermal decomposition — *1 mark*
b Copper carbonate → copper oxide + carbon dioxide — *2 marks*
Award one mark for the left-hand side and one mark for the right-hand side of the equation.

> **Note to parent**
>
> At Level 6 your child will be expected to write simple word equations. In this case it is a matter of using the information given.

c Less than 4 g — *1 mark*
d Magnesium joins with oxygen from the air when it burns — *1 mark*
Total 5 marks

> **Note to parent**
>
> Questions **8c** and **8d** are about mass changes with chemical reactions. In **c**, there is a mass loss because oxygen is lost. In **d**, there is a mass gain as oxygen is gained.

9 a Iron is a metal. — *1 mark*
Sulphur is a non-metal. — *1 mark*

> **Note to parent**
>
> The most reliable test to see if an element is a metal or non-metal is to burn the element in oxygen and then test the oxide formed. If the oxide is acidic (pH less than 7), the element is a non-metal. If the oxide is neutral or alkaline (pH of 7 or greater), the element is a metal.

b Use a magnet. — *1 mark*
Iron sticks to the magnet and can be removed. Sulphur does not. — *1 mark*

Test C Answers

Note to parent

Most pupils get the first mark but few go on to get the second. Probably in most cases they know the answer, and would give it if asked orally, but do not think to write it down. The question is worth two marks and they should be aware that 'use a magnet' is not a two-mark answer.

c	Iron sulphide	*1 mark*
d	A mixture of iron and sulphur – C	*1 mark*
	A compound of iron and sulphur – A	*1 mark*
		Total 7 marks

10 Darren's parents could be tall and he could have a better diet. *2 marks*
Total 2 marks

11 a Granite *1 mark*
b Marble *1 mark*
Total 2 marks

Note to parent

Granite is an igneous rock and marble is a metamorphic rock. Limestone is a sedimentary rock.

12 a A red-brown solid is formed (*or* deposited, *or* left on the electrode). *1 mark*

Note to parent

This solid is copper but your child does not have to identify it. Copper ions are discharged at the negative electrode during electrolysis.

b The blue colour fades. *1 mark*

Note to parent

This removal of the colour is caused by the removal of copper from the solution.

Total 2 marks

13 a The A should be placed between one side of the bulb and a black dot. *1 mark*

Note to parent

It does not matter which side of the bulb the ammeter is placed, since the current leaving the bulb is the same as the current that enters the bulb.

b The B should be placed between one side of the battery and a black dot. *1 mark*
Total 2 marks

14 a Speeding up – A *1 mark*
Slowing down – C and D *One mark each: 2 marks*
Travelling at a steady speed – B *1 mark*
b The resistive force or air resistance *1 mark*
c There is not enough friction between the wheels and the road. *1 mark*
Total 6 marks

Test C Answers

> **Note to parent**
>
> Children often get confused about forces that resist motion and they tend to use 'friction' to describe any resistive force. Friction is the force that opposes slipping or sliding.

15 a M's orbit is elliptical, V's is circular. *1 mark*
V's is longer or further from the Sun. *1 mark*

   b M
      E
      V
Three correct: 2 marks; two correct: 1 mark   *2 marks*
Total 4 marks

16 B and D   *One mark each: 2 marks*
Total 2 marks

> **Note to parent**
>
> The light in **B** is at right angles to the glass and so passes through without refraction. Your child may have missed this and just chosen **D** where refraction is shown. It is worth pointing out that, because two marks are available, two answers are expected.

17 C   *1 mark*
Total 1 mark

TOTAL FOR TEST C 65 marks

Determining your child's level

FINDING YOUR CHILD'S LEVEL IN TESTS A AND B

When you have marked a test, enter the total number of marks your child scored for each question on the Marking Grid overleaf. Then add them up and enter the test total on the grid.

Using the total for each test, look at the chart below to determine your child's level for each test.

Test A or Test B

Level 2 or below	Level 3	Level 4	Level 5
up to 19	20–32	33–59	60+

FINDING YOUR CHILD'S OVERALL LEVEL IN SCIENCE

After you have worked out separate levels for Tests A and B, add up your child's total marks for the two tests. Use this total and the chart below to determine your child's overall level in Science. The chart also shows you how your child's level in these tests compares with the target level for his or her age group.

Total for Tests A and B

Level 2 or below	Level 3	Level 4	Level 5
up to 38	39–64	65–118	119+
Working towards target level for age group		Working at target level	Working beyond target level

If your child achieved Level 5 in Tests A and B, you may want to see how he or she does on Test C. A score of 42 or higher on Test C indicates that your child is working beyond the target level, at Level 6.

Marking Grid

TEST A — Pages 1–19

Question	Marks available	Marks scored	Question	Marks available	Marks scored
1	11		12	3	
2	5		13	3	
3	9		14	3	
4	7		15	1	
5	3		16	2	
6	7		17	2	
7	3		18	6	
8	5		19	4	
9	4		20	2	
10	5		21	7	
11	8		Total	100	

TEST B — Pages 20–36

Question	Marks available	Marks scored	Question	Marks available	Marks scored
1	3		13	3	
2	6		14	6	
3	4		15	3	
4	7		16	2	
5	5		17	1	
6	5		18	2	
7	14		19	3	
8	3		20	1	
9	3		21	2	
10	7		22	3	
11	8		23	5	
12	4		Total	100	

TEST C — Pages 37–48

Question	Marks available	Marks scored	Question	Marks available	Marks scored
1	6		10	2	
2	6		11	2	
3	5		12	2	
4	6		13	2	
5	2		14	6	
6	1		15	4	
7	6		16	2	
8	5		17	1	
9	7		Total	65	